# Student Activity Journal

TEACHER'S EDITION

## ACCESS

### Building Literacy Through Learning™

# Science

**Great Source Education Group**

a division of Houghton Mifflin Company

Wilmington, Massachusetts

www.greatsource.com

## AUTHORS

**Dr. Elva Duran** holds a Ph.D. from the University of Oregon in special education and reading disabilities. Duran has been an elementary reading and middle school teacher in Texas and overseas. Currently, she is a professor in the Department of Special Education, Rehabilitation, and School Psychology at California State University, Sacramento, where she teaches beginning reading and language and literacy courses. Duran is co-author of the Leamos Español reading program and has published two textbooks, *Teaching Students with Moderate/Severe Disabilities* and *Systematic Instruction in Reading for Spanish-Speaking Students*.

**Jo Gusman** grew up in a family of migrants and knows firsthand the complexities surrounding a second-language learner. Gusman's career in bilingual education began in 1974. In 1981, she joined the staff of the Newcomer School in Sacramento. There she developed her brain-based ESL strategies. Her work has garnered national television appearances and awards, including the Presidential Recognition for Excellence in Teaching. Gusman is the author of *Practical Strategies for Accelerating the Literacy Skills and Content Learning of Your ESL Students*. She is a featured video presenter, including "Multiple Intelligences and the Second Language Learner." Currently, she teaches at California State University, Sacramento, and at the Multiple Intelligences Institute at the University of California, Riverside.

**Dr. John Shefelbine** is a professor in the Department of Teacher Education, California State University, Sacramento. His degrees include a Master of Arts in Teaching in reading and language arts, K–12, from Harvard University and a Ph.D. in educational psychology from Stanford University. During his 11 years as an elementary and middle school teacher, Shefelbine has worked with students from linguistically and culturally diverse populations in Alaska, Arizona, Idaho, and New Mexico. Shefelbine was a contributor to the California Reading Language Arts Framework, the California Reading Initiative, and the California Reading and Literature Project, and has authored a variety of reading materials and programs for developing fluent, confident readers.

EDITORIAL: Developed by Nieman Inc. with Phil LaLeike
DESIGN: Ronan Design

Printed in the United States of America

International Standard Book Number -13: 978-0-669-50901-4
International Standard Book Number -10: 0-669-50901-9
*(Student Activity Journal)*

4 5 6 7 8 9-2266-18 17 16 15 14 13 12

International Standard Book Number -13: 978-0-669-51660-9
International Standard Book Number -10: 0-669-51660-0
*(Student Activity Journal, Teacher's Edition)*

6 7 8 9-2266-17 16 15

4500519076

## CONSULTANTS

**Shane Bassett**
Mill Park Elementary School
David Douglas School District
Portland, OR

**Jeanette Gordon**
Senior Educational Consultant
Illinois Resource Center
Des Plaines, IL

**Dr. Aixa Perez-Prado**
College of Education
Florida International University
Miami, FL

**Dennis Terdy**
Director of Grants
  and Special Programs
Newcomer Center
Township High School
Arlington Heights, IL

## TEACHER GROUP REVIEWERS

**Sara Ainsworth**
Hannah Beardsley
  Middle School
Crystal Lake, IL

**Walter A. Blair**
Otis Elementary School
Chicago, IL

**Vincent U. Egonmwan**
Joyce Kilmer
  Elementary School
Chicago, IL

**Anne Hopkins**
Arie Crown School
Skokie, IL

**Heather Pusich**
Field Middle School
Northbrook, IL

**Dana Robinson**
Prairie Crossing
  Charter School
Grayslake, IL

**Nestor Torres**
Chase Elementary School
Chicago, IL

## RESEARCH SITE LEADERS

**Carmen Concepción**
Lawton Chiles Middle School
Miami, FL

**Andrea Dabbs**
Edendale Middle School
San Lorenzo, CA

**Daniel Garcia**
Public School 130
Bronx, NY

**Bobbi Ciriza Houtchens**
Arroyo Valley High School
San Bernardino, CA

**Portia McFarland**
Wendell Phillips High School
Chicago, IL

## RESEARCH SITE SCIENCE REVIEWERS

**Kristen Can**
Edendale Middle School
San Lorenzo, CA

**Delores King**
Warren Elementary School
Chicago, IL

**Dania E. Lima**
Lawton Chiles Middle School
Miami, FL

**Elizabeth Tremberger**
Bronx, NY

**Jackie Womack**
Martin Luther King, Jr.
  Middle School
San Bernardino, CA

## SCIENCE TEACHER REVIEWERS

**Said Salah Ahmed**
Sanford Middle School
Minneapolis, MN

**Kellie A. Danzinger**
Carpentersville Middle School
Carpentersville, IL

**Jean E. Garrity**
Washington Middle School
Kenosha, WI

**Jon L. Kimsey**
Carpenter
  Elementary School
Chicago, IL

**Anna Kong**
Stone Academy
Chicago, IL

**Jill McCarthy**
Auburndale, MA

**Donna O'Neill**
Luther Jackson
  Middle School
Falls Church, VA

**Kevin Smith**
North Welcome Center
Columbus, OH

**Nancy Svendsen**
J. E. B. Stuart School
Falls Church, VA

**Jill M. Thompson**
Roosevelt Middle School
Blaine, MN

ACKNOWLEDGMENTS
**Cover Credits:** *Foreground:* frog: © Getty Images; prism: © Getty Images; stars: © Photodisc/Getty Images *Background:* © Photodisc/Getty Images; © BrandX/Getty Images. Based on a system of labeling the columns A through J and the rows 1 through 18, the following background images were taken by the following photographers: A8, A10, A13, A16, A18, C9, C11, C13, C14, C16, C17, D5, D7, D8, D11, D13, D15, D18, E1, E8, E12, E15, E16, E17, E19, E20, F1, F2, F5, F6, F11, F13, F17, F19, G9, G10, G12, H2, H3, H12, H13, H17, I1, I8, I9, I11, I14, I16, I18, I19, J2, J4, J5, J6, J8, J12, J13, J17, J19: Philip Coblentz/Getty Images; A5, E7: Steve Allen/Getty Images; F16: Sexto Sol/Getty Images; B19: Spike Mafford/Getty Images; B12: Philippe Colombi/Getty Images; J1: Albert J Copley/Getty Images
**Photo Credits: 4** *top* © Eileen Ryan Photography, 2004 *center right* © Royalty-Free/CORBIS *bottom* © Eileen Ryan Photography, 2004 **5** *top* © Getty Images *center right* © Eileen Ryan Photography, 2004 *bottom* © Eileen Ryan Photography, 2004 **104** © Charles D. Winters/Photo Researchers, Inc. **105** © Getty Images **106** © Eileen Ryan Photography, 2004 **107** © Royalty-Free/CORBIS **108** © Eileen Ryan Photography, 2004 **110** © Getty Images
**Illustration Credits: 96** © Jonathan Massie

# TABLE OF

# CONTENTS

# Being a Scientist

**My Word List**

**A. Word Web** As you study Lesson 1 in *ACCESS Science*, complete the Word Web below with vocabulary words from the lesson. In the ovals, write words that describe parts of the science process.

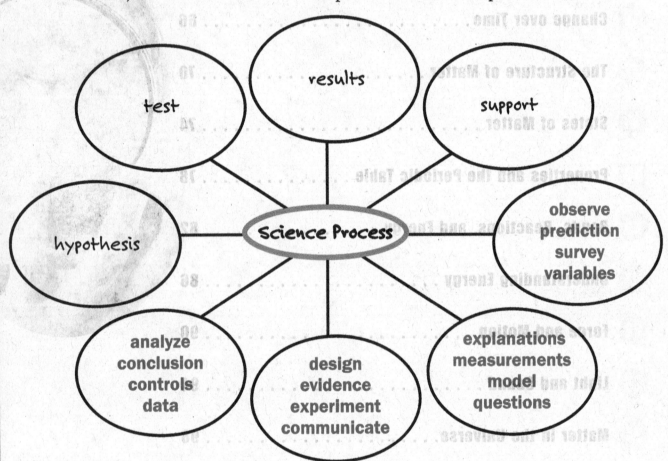

**B. Writing Sentences** Write 2–3 sentences describing how parts of the science process relate to one another. Use at least 3 words from your Word Web.

*Answers will vary. Look for an underlying understanding*

*that questions lead to tests, which lead to conclusions and*

*more questions.*

_____

_____

**Skill Building**

**A. Use the Science Process** After you study the lesson, use the space below to draw the steps of the bouncing ball experiment in order. Use the information on page 19. Then use your pictures to explain the experiment to a partner.

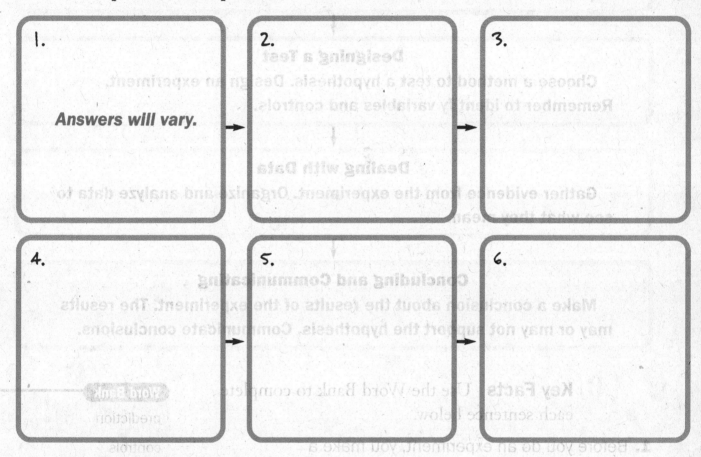

1.

*Answers will vary.*

2.

3.

4.

5.

6.

**B. Choosing Vocabulary** In each sentence below, underline the word that best completes the sentence.

**1.** I use my (explanations, <u>senses</u>) to observe the world.

**2.** (<u>Variables</u>, Results) are things that can affect what happens in an experiment.

**3.** Many times, (survey, <u>technology</u>) makes work easier.

**4.** I need to (support, <u>analyze</u>) my data before I can write a conclusion.

**5.** If scientists don't (<u>communicate</u>, affect), they cannot ask new questions.

## My Study Notes

### A. Study Skill: Using Process Notes
Complete the Process Notes for Lesson 1. Use information under each heading in *ACCESS Science* to write notes in the boxes. *Sample answer:*

**From Question to Hypothesis**

Observe the world and ask questions. Think of possible explanations and make predictions.

↓

**Designing a Test**

Choose a method to test a hypothesis. Design an experiment. Remember to identify variables and controls.

↓

**Dealing with Data**

Gather evidence from the experiment. Organize and analyze data to see what they mean.

↓

**Concluding and Communicating**

Make a conclusion about the results of the experiment. The results may or may not support the hypothesis. Communicate conclusions.

### B. Key Facts
Use the Word Bank to complete each sentence below.

**Word Bank**
prediction
controls
analyze
variable

**1.** Before you do an experiment, you make a
____**prediction**____ about what will happen.

**2.** As you design your experiment, you identify a single
____**variable**____, or the factor that will change.

**3.** To get accurate results, your experiment must have ____**controls**____,
or factors that stay the same.

**4.** When you ____**analyze**____ data, you decide what they mean.

## Showing What I Know

**Relating**  Kim conducted an experiment to test this hypothesis: *Jackie will eat cheese faster than broccoli.* Think about the evidence in the chart below. Then write a possible explanation.

| Evidence | | Explanation |
|---|---|---|
| **Food** | **Eating Speed** | *Answers will vary, but should show that Jackie ate broccoli faster.* |
| cheese | 10 minutes | |
| broccoli | 5 minutes | |

Think about the organizer above and then write 1–3 sentences to relate the evidence and your explanation. Be sure to say whether or not the results support the hypothesis.

_The evidence did not support the hypothesis because Jackie ate_

_broccoli faster than cheese._

_____

_____

_____

_____

## My Summary of the Lesson

*Sample answer:*

**Scientists ask questions about the world and make predictions. They perform experiments to test their hypotheses and talk about the results with other scientists.**

# Understanding Earth

**My Word List**

### A. Definition Web
Complete this Definition Web about the structure of Earth. Write the meaning of each word in the box.

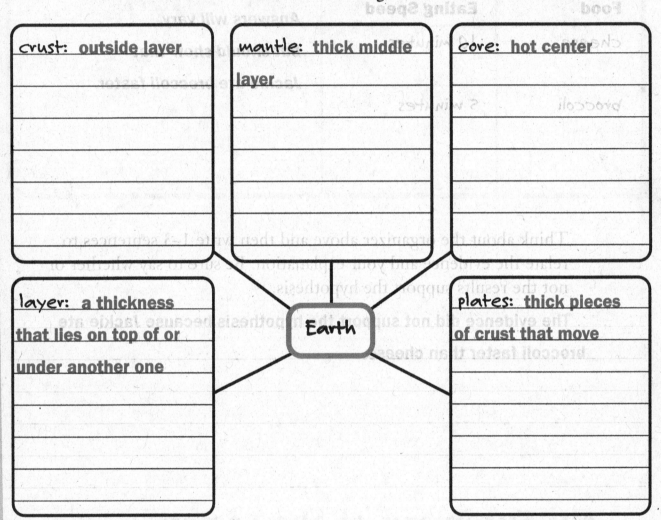

crust: **outside layer**

mantle: **thick middle layer**

core: **hot center**

Earth

layer: **a thickness that lies on top of or under another one**

plates: **thick pieces of crust that move**

### B. Sentence Frame
Use the words in your Definition Web to complete the paragraph below.

Earth has 3 main layers. We live on the top _____**layer**_____.
This outside layer, with the oceans and continents, is called
the _____**crust**_____. Underneath the oceans and continents are
_____**plates**_____ that move. The thick middle layer of Earth is the
_____**mantle**_____. The hot center of Earth is the _____**core**_____.

**Skill Building**

**A. Analyze Evidence**  After you read the lesson, fill in this Web about earthquakes. In each oval, write one piece of evidence showing how earthquakes happen. *Sample answer:*

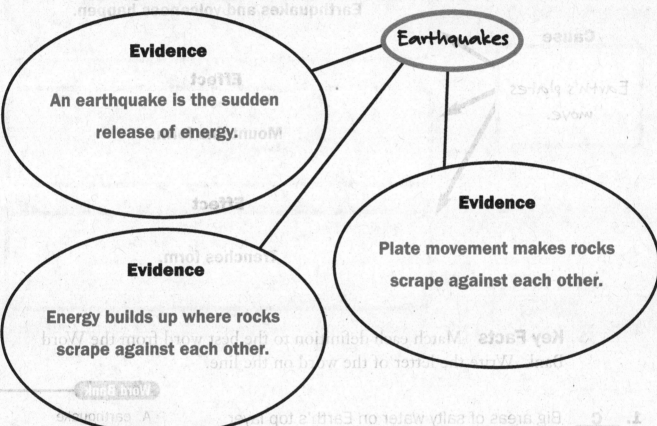

**Evidence**

An earthquake is the sudden release of energy.

**Earthquakes**

**Evidence**

Plate movement makes rocks scrape against each other.

**Evidence**

Energy builds up where rocks scrape against each other.

**B. Writing Sentences**  Use details from your Web to write 2–3 sentences analyzing your evidence. Tell how your evidence explains why the ground shakes during an earthquake.

*Sample answer:*

*When two plates scrape together, energy builds up until the*

*rock breaks. When this happens, energy is released. This makes*

*the ground shake.*

## My Study Notes

**A.** **Study Skill: Using a Cause-Effect Organizer**  As you study the lesson, complete this Cause-Effect Organizer about plate tectonics. In the boxes, write 3 effects caused by moving plates.

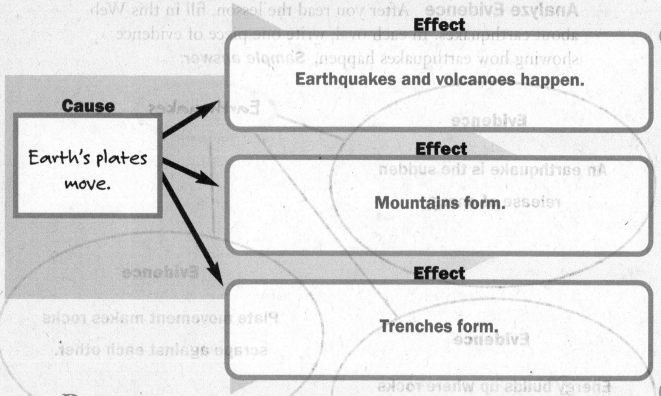

**Cause**

Earth's plates move.

**Effect**

Earthquakes and volcanoes happen.

**Effect**

Mountains form.

**Effect**

Trenches form.

**B.** **Key Facts**  Match each definition to the best word from the Word Bank. Write the letter of the word on the line.

**Word Bank**

A. earthquake
B. volcano
C. oceans
D. mountains
E. trenches
F. continents

1. __C__  Big areas of salty water on Earth's top layer
2. __F__  Large areas of land on Earth's crust
3. __D__  Form when Earth's surface wrinkles
4. __E__  Deep, low areas in the bottoms of oceans
5. __B__  Happens when melted rock comes out of Earth
6. __A__  Happens when the ground shakes

**Name**

## Showing What I Know

**Summarizing** In the box, draw a picture to show evidence that volcanoes let hot rock out of Earth. Label your picture. Then, on the lines, write a summary of the evidence shown in your picture.

*Students' pictures should resemble the diagram on page 36 of ACCESS Science and have these labels: magma, lava, and volcano. Other labels may be included.*

Sample answer:

Rock that is hot rises inside a volcano. Magma comes through the volcano and out of the top. When it comes out, it is called lava. Lava is hot until it cools.

# My Summary of the Lesson

Sample answer:

Earth has three layers: the mantle, crust, and core. Hot rock inside Earth becomes soft and moves plates. When plates move, they can cause earthquakes and volcanoes.

# All About Rocks

## My Word List

**A. Complete the Diagram**  As you read the lesson, complete this diagram with vocabulary words that describe parts of the rock cycle.

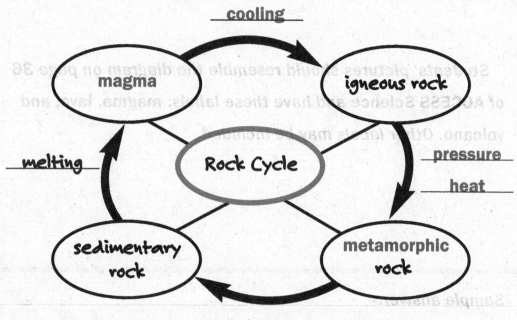

cooling

magma

igneous rock

melting

Rock Cycle

pressure

heat

sedimentary rock

metamorphic rock

weathering

**B. Writing Sentences**  Write 2–3 sentences explaining how the rock cycle works. Use at least 3 words from your Web.

The 3 kinds of rock are sedimentary, igneous, and metamorphic. The rock cycle shows how each kind of rock can change into a different kind. Heat, pressure, and weathering can cause these changes.

### Skill Building

**Make Observations**   In the box, draw one of the kinds of rocks shown on page 41 of *ACCESS Science*. Include as many details as you can in your picture. Next, study your picture carefully. Then, write your observations about this kind of rock on the lines below.

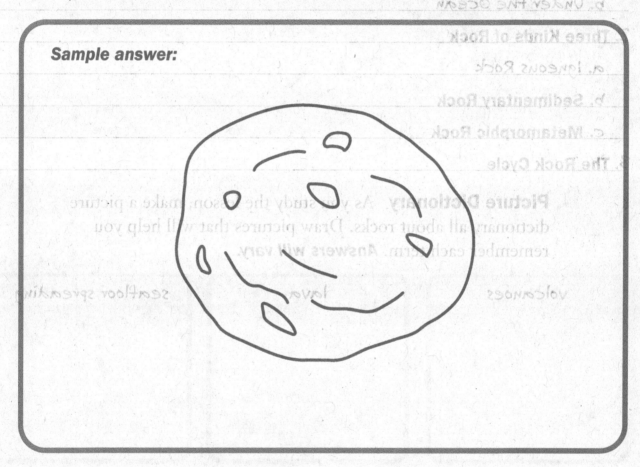

**Sample answer:**

Observations *Sample answer for igneous rock:*

1. **The rock is pink with black and white spots in it.**

2. **It is smooth.**

3. **It looks like different kinds of rock melted together.**

## My Study Notes

**A.** **Study Skill: Outlining the Lesson** Complete a study outline of this lesson. Use the headings on pages 44–49 of *ACCESS Science* to fill in the blanks.

1. Where Rock Forms _____
    a. On Land _____
    b. Under the Ocean _____

2. **Three Kinds of Rock** _____
    a. **Igneous Rock** _____
    b. **Sedimentary Rock** _____
    c. **Metamorphic Rock** _____

3. **The Rock Cycle** _____

**B.** **Picture Dictionary** As you study the lesson, make a picture dictionary all about rocks. Draw pictures that will help you remember each term. *Answers will vary.*

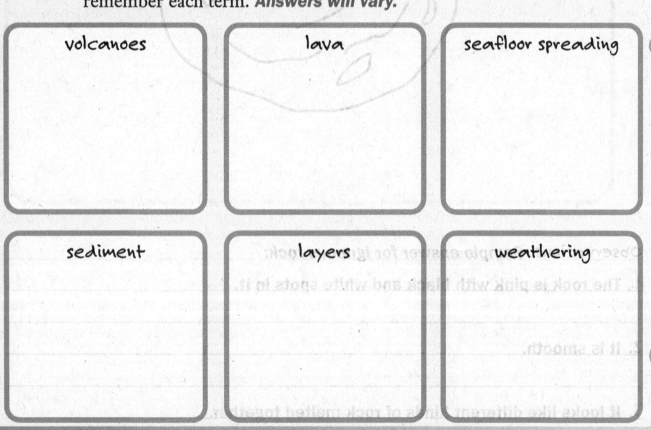

| volcanoes | lava | seafloor spreading |
| sediment | layers | weathering |

### Showing What I Know

**A. Interpreting** Look at page 46 in *ACCESS Science* and study the rock the boy is holding. In the first column, write your observations about the rock. What kind of rock is it? Write your interpretation in the second column. *Sample answer:*

**Topic:** Rocks

| Observations | Interpretations |
|---|---|
| 1. The rock contains a shark's tooth. | This is a sedimentary rock. |
| 2. The rock looks rough. | |
| 3. The rock has different colors. | |

**B. Writing Sentences** Use the details in your Observation Journal to write 2–3 sentences explaining your interpretation.

*Sample answer:*

I can tell this is a sedimentary rock because it has a shark's tooth. I know that sedimentary rock contains small pieces of rock, shells, and bone.

## My Summary of the Lesson

*Sample answer:*

There are three kinds of rock, called igneous, sedimentary, and metamorphic. The rock cycle shows how one kind of rock can turn into any other kind of rock.

# The Changing Surface of Earth

**My Word List**

**A. Definition Chart**  Find these words in the lesson. Write the definition and use the word in a sentence.

| Word | Definition | Example Sentence |
|---|---|---|
| weathering | the process of rock being broken apart | Weathering can change the surface of Earth. |
| erosion | the process of rock moving from place to place | A beach changes shape because of erosion. |
| deposition | the process of putting down rock | Deposition puts rock down in a new place. |
| expand | get larger | Freezing water can expand and break rocks apart. |

**B. Choosing Vocabulary**  Read each sentence below. Then underline the word that best completes the sentence.

1. (Deposition, <u>Erosion</u>) moves rock from one place to another.
2. Chemical (<u>weathering</u>, deposition) changes the chemicals inside rock.
3. Gravity affects (<u>deposition</u>, expand).
4. Ice can cause a crack in rock to (weather, <u>expand</u>).

**Skill Building**

**A. Organize Data** Mechanical weathering can be caused by water and by living things. As you study pages 56–57 in *ACCESS Science*, fill in this Venn Diagram with facts about these weathering causes. Put differences in the outside parts. Put similarities in the overlapping part. *Sample answer:*

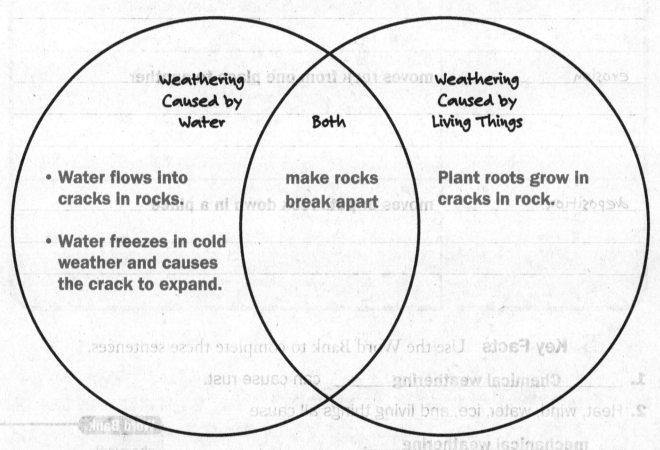

Weathering Caused by Water

Both

Weathering Caused by Living Things

- Water flows into cracks in rocks.

- Water freezes in cold weather and causes the crack to expand.

make rocks break apart

Plant roots grow in cracks in rock.

**B. Writing Sentences** Use the details from your Venn Diagram to write 2–3 sentences telling how the two kinds of mechanical weathering are alike and different. *Sample answer:*

Both kinds of weathering break rock into smaller pieces. Both kinds cause cracks to become larger. Weathering caused by water happens when water freezes in cracks. Weathering caused by living things happens when plants grow in cracks.

**My Study Notes**

**A. Study Skill: Using Key Word or Topic Notes**  As you study the lesson, complete these Key Word or Topic Notes. Use information under the headings in your book for help.

| Key Words or Topics | Notes |
|---|---|
| weathering | wind, rain, ice, and other ways rock breaks apart |
| erosion | moves rock from one place to another |
| deposition | moves or puts rock down in a place |

**B. Key Facts**  Use the Word Bank to complete these sentences.

1. _____Chemical weathering_____ can cause rust.

2. Heat, wind, water, ice, and living things all cause

   _____mechanical weathering_____.

3. A _____landslide_____ can be caused by just one rock slipping out of place.

4. Over thousands of years, _____glaciers_____ can make U-shaped valleys in Earth's surface.

**Word Bank**

chemical
   weathering

landslide

mechanical
   weathering

glaciers

## Showing What I Know

**Comparing and Contrasting** In the boxes below, draw a picture of a landslide and a picture of a flood. Below write two sentences that explain how landslides and floods are alike and different.

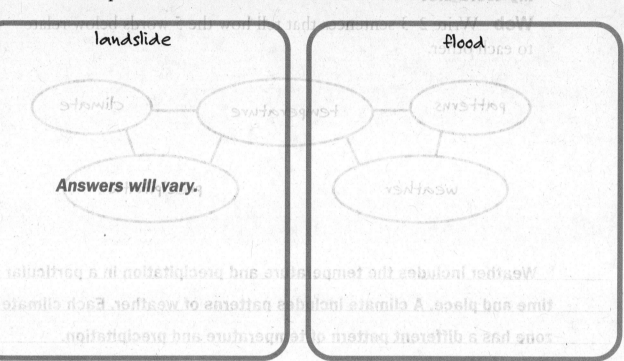

landslide

flood

Answers will vary.

_Sample answer:_

A landslide moves rocks down a mountain. A flood washes soil away from a field. Both landslides and floods can make fast changes in Earth's surface. Landslides happen because of gravity, and floods happen because of fast-moving water.

# My Summary of the Lesson

_Sample answer:_

Wind, water, gravity, and living things change the surface of Earth. Weathering, erosion, and deposition are 3 ways the surface of Earth changes.

# Climate and Weather

### My Word List

**A. Web** Write 2–3 sentences that tell how the 5 words below relate to each other.

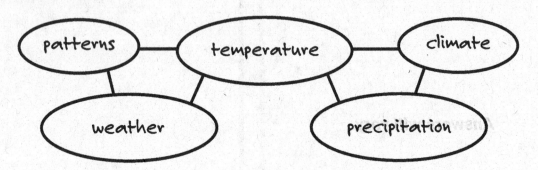

_Weather includes the temperature and precipitation in a particular_

_time and place. A climate includes patterns of weather. Each climate_

_zone has a different pattern of temperature and precipitation._

_____

_____

_____

_____

**B. Sentence Frame** Use words from your Web to complete the sentences below. Then read the conversation aloud with a partner.

**Maria:** What do you think the weather will be like tomorrow?

**Therese:** I heard the _____**temperature**_____ will go up to 107 degrees!

**Maria:** Wow! We have very hot _____**weather**_____ here in the summer.

**Therese:** Sometimes it cools off a little after we get rain or other _____**precipitation**_____.

**Name** _____

**Skill Building**

A. **Look for Patterns**  Look at the temperatures and precipitation in this Weather Chart. Find the biggest change or changes in each row and circle where they are.

| | MON | TUES | WED | THURS | FRI | SAT | SUN |
|---|---|---|---|---|---|---|---|
| **High Temperature** | 86 °F | 84 °F | 71 °F | 75 °F | 77 °F | 75 °F | 76 °F |
| **Low Temperature** | 65 °F | 60 °F | 53 °F | 53 °F | 58 °F | 57 °F | 57°F |
| **Precipitation and Clouds** | none | cloudy | cloudy | cloudy | rain | cloudy | rain |

B. **Writing Sentences**  Now use the details from your Weather Chart to write 2–3 sentences describing the changes and how they affect any pattern you see.

_Sample answer:_

**The high temperature dropped from the 80s to the 70s in**

**the middle of the week, and the low temperature dropped from**

**the 60s to the 50s. A few days after this change, it rained.**

**Temperatures in the 70s seem to come with clouds or rain.**

_____

_____

Name _____

**My Study Notes**

**A.** **Study Skill: Using Sequence Notes** Use information on pages 70–71 of *ACCESS Science* to complete these Sequence Notes about the water cycle. Remember to use signal words such as *next*, *then*, and *after*.

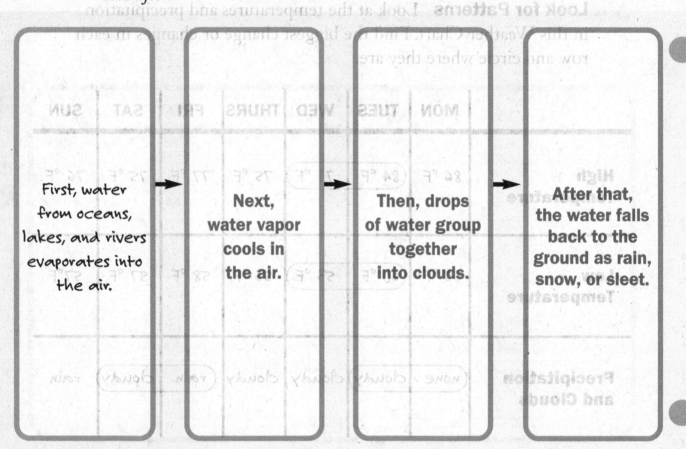

First, water from oceans, lakes, and rivers evaporates into the air. → Next, water vapor cools in the air. → Then, drops of water group together into clouds. → After that, the water falls back to the ground as rain, snow, or sleet.

**B.** **Key Facts** Use the Word Bank to match each definition to the word it describes. Write the letter of the word on the line.

**Word Bank**
A. humidity
B. tropical
C. precipitation
D. temperate
E. solar energy
F. hurricane

1. __E__ Warms the surface of Earth
2. __C__ Can be in the form of fog, rain, snow, or sleet
3. __B__ The climate zone that is near the equator
4. __F__ A kind of storm that starts over the ocean
5. __D__ Climate zones with both hot and cold seasons
6. __A__ Measure of how much water is in the air

**Name** _____

FOR USE WITH PAGE 74

## Showing What I Know

**A. Predicting** Draw 3 pictures that show the weather in your area for 3 days in a row. Then study your pictures. What do you think the weather will be like on day 4? Draw a picture in the last box to show your prediction.

| Day 1 | Day 2 |
|---|---|
| *Answers will vary.* | |

| Day 3 | Day 4: My Prediction |
|---|---|
| | |

**B. My Word Bank** On the lines below, make a Word Bank that includes the words you need to describe your pictures. Then use the words to explain your weather prediction to a partner.

*Words may include*
temperature, precipitation
(*or* rain, fog, snow, sleet), dry,
cloudy, sunny, *and* gloomy.

# My Summary of the Lesson

*Sample answer:*
Energy from the sun creates different climate zones on Earth. It also affects weather patterns and the water cycle.

# Earth, Sun, and Moon

**My Word List**

**A. Definition Chart** Find these words on pages 78–85 of *ACCESS Science*. Write the definition and use each word in a sentence.

| Word | Definition | Example Sentence |
|---|---|---|
| rotates | turns or spins in place | Earth rotates on its axis. |
| axis | an imaginary line through the center of something | Earth's axis goes straight through Earth's center. |
| revolves | travels in a path around something | Earth revolves around the sun. |
| orbits | revolves in a way that is controlled by gravity | The moon orbits Earth. |
| tilted | slanted | Part of Earth is always tilted toward the sun. |

**B. Choosing Vocabulary** In each sentence below, underline the word that best completes the sentence.

**1.** We have day and night because Earth (revolves, <u>rotates</u>) on its axis.

**2.** Earth's (<u>axis</u>, orbits) goes straight through the North Pole and the South Pole.

**3.** We have seasons because Earth (rotates, <u>revolves</u>) around the sun.

**4.** As the moon (<u>orbits</u>, rotates) Earth, we see different parts of the moon's surface.

**5.** It is summer in your town when your part of Earth is (axis, <u>tilted</u>) toward the sun.

## Skill Building

**A. Use a Model** In the box below, draw a picture to show the positions of Earth and the sun when it is 12:00 noon in your town. Use the pictures and information on pages 80–81 of *ACCESS Science* for help.

> *Students' pictures will vary. No matter how students show the town and the light source, the drawings should show their part of Earth completely facing the sun. Earth may be tilted according to your season.*

**B. Writing Sentences** Now use the details from your picture to write 1–3 sentences explaining what your model shows.

<u>**During the day, our part of Earth completely faces the sun. The**</u>
<u>**sun appears highest in the sky at noon. On the opposite side of**</u>
<u>**Earth, it is the middle of the night (midnight).**</u>

## My Study Notes

**A. Study Skill: Outlining the Lesson**   Complete a study outline of this lesson. Use the headings in *ACCESS Science* to fill in the blanks.

1. Day and Night

    a. Rotation

    b. **Day Starts**

    c. **Day Ends**

2. Seasons

    a. **Summer and Winter**

    b. Spring and Fall

3. **The Moon**

    a. Moon and Sun

    b. **Tides**

4. Eclipses

    a. **Solar Eclipses**

    b. **Lunar Eclipses**

**B. Key Facts**   Use the Word Bank to complete these sentences.

**1.** Summer, winter, spring, and fall are the 4 _____**seasons**_____.

**2.** Tides are caused mostly by the gravity of the _____**moon**_____.

**3.** The terms *waxing crescent* and *waning gibbous* refer to two of the moon's _____**phases**_____.

**4.** In a ___**solar eclipse**___, the moon partly blocks the sun's light on Earth.

**5.** When Earth makes a shadow on the moon, the event is called a ___**lunar eclipse**___.

**Word Bank**

solar eclipse

phases

lunar eclipse

seasons

moon

## Showing What I Know

**Describing**   In the space below, draw a model of a lunar eclipse. Include the positions of the sun, moon, and Earth in your picture. Then on the lines, write sentences to describe your model and tell what it shows.

> *Students' models should show Earth between the moon and sun so that Earth casts a shadow on the moon.*

*Sample answer:*

My model shows the sun, moon, and Earth. Earth is between the moon and the sun. Earth makes a shadow on the moon. This is what happens in a lunar eclipse.

# My Summary of the Lesson

*Sample answer:*

The sun, moon, and Earth are a system. The way they move causes day and night, the seasons, and eclipses.

# Natural Resources

**My Word List**

## A. What Is It?
Below, write a sentence that tells what each word means and how it relates to the world around you.

*Sample answer:*

(resource) — A resource is anything we use to help make life better. _____

(renewable) — Water is a renewable resource. _____

(renew) — We can renew some resources by using them again. _____

(nonrenewable) — We may run out of nonrenewable resources. _____

(conserving) — Conserving resources helps them last longer. _____

## B. Sentence Frame
Use the words above to complete the paragraph below.

A natural _____resource_____ is something people use to make energy, grow food, or build things. The wind and the sun are _____renewable_____ resources. Coal and oil are _____nonrenewable_____ resources, which means we may run out of them. _____Conserving_____ nonrenewable resources will help them last longer. Recycling is one way to do this. Each time that you recycle a drink can you _____renew_____ a resource!

**Name** _____

**Skill Building**

**A.** **Use Math to Organize Data**  Conduct a survey to find out how the people in your class dry their hair after washing it. What percentage of your class uses energy from electricity (a hair dryer) and what percentage uses energy from wind and air? Fill in and label the pie chart below to show your data. Use the steps on page 91 of *ACCESS Science* to complete your chart.

*Answers will depend on survey results. You may do a class survey by having students raise their hands for hair dryer, wind and air, and "other." Give students time to count and record responses.*

**B.** **My Word Bank**  Write the words and phrases you need to explain the data in your pie chart. Then explain your chart to a partner.

_Answers should include the_ _____

_word percent or percentage._ _____

_____    _____

_____    _____

_____    _____

## My Study Notes

**A. Study Skill: Using a Main Idea Organizer** As you study the lesson, use pages 92–97 of *ACCESS Science* to complete this Main Idea Organizer about natural resources. Write notes about each detail in the boxes. Then write a sentence to tell your conclusion.

**Main Idea:** People use natural resources to help make life better.

| Detail | Detail | Detail |
|---|---|---|
| Renewable Resources | Nonrenewable Resources | Conserving Resources |
| Wind, sun, and water resources are renewable because they will never run out. | Fossil fuels and nuclear energy are nonrenewable because we may run out of them. | We can conserve by using more renewable resources like hydroelectric power. |

**My Conclusion:** People should use resources wisely.

**B. Key Facts** Use the Word Bank to match each sentence with the resource it describes. Write the letter of the resource on the line.

1. __C__ This is all the renewable resources that come from living things.

2. __B__ Oil and coal are two examples of these resources.

3. __A__ This kind of energy comes from a change to the atoms in uranium.

4. __F__ This type of fossil fuel is invisible.

5. __E__ This renewable resource can only be used where there is heat inside Earth.

6. __D__ Water wheels can help create this renewable resource.

**Word Bank**

A. nuclear energy

B. fossil fuels

C. biomass

D. hydroelectric power

E. geothermal energy

F. natural gas

**Name** _____

## Showing What I Know

**Summarizing**   This pie chart shows the energy resources for Powertown. First, fill in the key. Write the percentage of each energy resource on its line in the key. Then, write one or two sentences to summarize how much of Powertown's energy comes from renewable and nonrenewable resources.

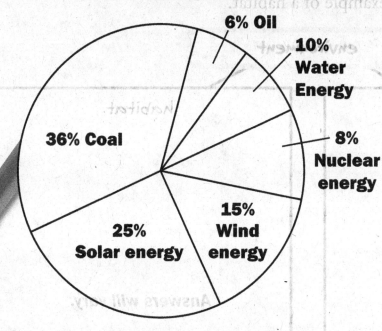

**Energy Resources for Powertown**

| **Key** | | |
|---|---|---|
| Coal | **36** % |
| Solar energy | **25** % |
| Wind energy | **15** % |
| Water energy | **10** % |
| Nuclear energy | **8** % |
| Oil | **6** % |

### My Data Summary

Powertown gets 50% of its energy from renewable resources and 50% from nonrenewable resources.

## My Summary of the Lesson

*Sample answer:*

Renewable resources are never used up. Nonrenewable resources can get used up. We conserve resources so that they last longer.

# How People Affect Earth

**My Word List**

### A. Word Pictures
Use the spaces below to draw the global environment and an example of a habitat.

environment

global

**Students should show all of Earth.**

habitat

**Answers will vary.**

### B. Writing Sentences
Write 2–3 sentences to explain each of your drawings.

Sample answer:

**The global environment covers Earth and includes many different habitats. Every living thing has its own habitat.**

**Skill Building**

**A. Infer from Evidence** Fill in the chart below to show two examples of recycling in your neighborhood. Think about where your family and neighbors put different kinds of trash. Write observations in the first column. Then use what you already know, plus your observations, to write your inference in the second column.

### Topic: Recycling in my neighborhood

| Evidence (observations) | Inference |
|---|---|
| *Answers will vary, but should focus on the topic of recycling and list at least two items of evidence.* | *Inferences should reflect some thought about how much or how effectively people in the neighborhood recycle.* |

**B. Writing Sentences** Use the evidence from your chart to think about ways you can improve recycling in your neighborhood. Write 2–3 sentences to tell your suggestions.

*Students' answers will vary but should focus on suggestions for local recycling.*

**Name**

FOR USE WITH PAGES 104–109

## My Study Notes

**A. Study Skill: Using Key Word or Topic Notes** Complete the Key Word or Topic Notes below for this lesson. Use the information under the headings in *ACCESS Science*.

| Key Words or Topics | Notes |
|---|---|
| Where people live | **People live in different habitats. Most of the time, they live near water. There are about 6,300,000,000 people on Earth.** |
| Pollution | **Garbage is one form of pollution. Pesticides are another. Cars can pollute the air.** |
| Global climate change | **This means that Earth's climate is slowly getting a little warmer.** |
| Helping earth | **We can help Earth by recycling and protecting habitats.** |

**B. Key Facts** Use the Word Bank to complete these sentences.

**Word Bank**
greenhouse gases
population
pollution
conserve

1. Many cities have a ____population____ of more than a million people.

2. Most air ____pollution____ is caused by cars and other motor vehicles.

3. _Greenhouse gases_ stop some of Earth's heat from leaving the atmosphere.

4. You can ____conserve____ water by turning it off while you brush your teeth.

© GREAT SOURCE. ALL RIGHTS RESERVED.

**Showing What I Know**

**Explaining** Fill in this Web to make an inference about how pollution affects your habitat. Think about things people do that are harmful to the land, water, and air. Write evidence in the 3 circles. Then write your inference. **Sample answer:**

**My Inference**

Pollution from factories is harmful to wildlife and people.

**Evidence**
Factory waste dumped in streams and rivers pollutes drinking water.

**Evidence**
Gases from factories can make the air difficult to breathe.

**Evidence**
Animal habitats are often destroyed when factories pollute the land nearby.

Write 3–4 sentences that state your inference and explain it. Tell how the evidence supports your conclusion.

*Students should explain the connections between their evidence and their inference.*

# My Summary of the Lesson

**Sample answer:**
People change the land, air, and water where they live. People can harm Earth, but they also can help Earth.

# Exploring Ecology

**My Word List**

**A. Definition Chart**  Find these words in the lesson. Then write the definition and use the word in a sentence.

| Word | Definition | Example Sentence |
|------|------------|------------------|
| ecology | the science of how living things and their environments interact | The way birds build nests is part of ecology. |
| interact | affect one another | Lions that hunt an animal interact with that animal. |
| ecosystem | an environment and everything that lives in it | Soil, air, and sunlight are parts of an ecosystem. |
| species | a group of similar living things that can reproduce | Ants and flies are not the same species. |
| community | populations of different species living in the same environment | A community in a pond includes many species of fish. |

**B. Choosing Vocabulary**  Underline the word that best completes each sentence below.

1. The science of living things and their environments is called (ecology, ecosystem).

2. Plants and animals (interact, community) with one another in an ecosystem.

3. A (community, ecology) is made up of different species living in one environment.

4. Cactus plants and snakes are parts of a desert (ecosystem, species).

5. Every plant and animal is a member of a (species, ecology).

**Skill Building**

**A. Think About Systems** Use the information on page 116 of
*ACCESS Science* to complete this Web showing the parts of a
desert ecosystem. Include both living and nonliving things.

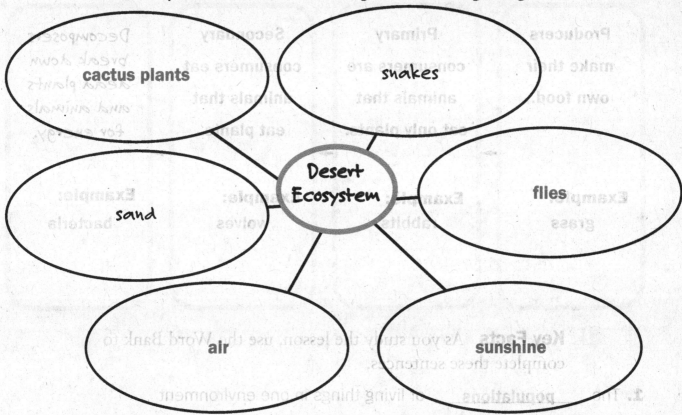

cactus plants

snakes

sand

Desert Ecosystem

flies

air

sunshine

**B. Writing Sentences** Use the words from your Web to write 2–3
sentences that tell how the parts of a desert ecosystem work together.

*Sample answer:*

**Cactus plants use the energy in sunshine to grow. Snakes rest on**

**the sand. Flies move through the air.**

**My Study Notes**

## A. Study Skill: Using Sequence Notes
Use the information on page 120 of *ACCESS Science* to complete the Sequence Notes below. Write the definition of each group and give an example.

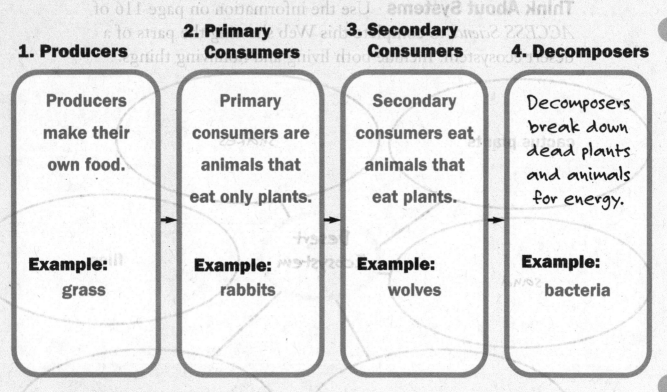

**1. Producers**

Producers make their own food.

Example: grass

**2. Primary Consumers**

Primary consumers are animals that eat only plants.

Example: rabbits

**3. Secondary Consumers**

Secondary consumers eat animals that eat plants.

Example: wolves

**4. Decomposers**

Decomposers break down dead plants and animals for energy.

Example: bacteria

## B. Key Facts
As you study the lesson, use the Word Bank to complete these sentences.

**1.** The ___populations___ of living things in one environment make up a community.

**2.** Sunlight provides the _____energy_____ that makes life in an ecosystem possible.

**3.** ___Nutrients___ give plants and animals the energy they need to live and grow.

**4.** During the carbon _____cycle_____, animals eat carbon in plants and release carbon dioxide.

**5.** Energy moves from producer plants to consumer animals in a _____food chain_____.

**Word Bank**

nutrients

cycle

populations

food chain

energy

### Showing What I Know

**Explaining**  In the box, draw a picture of the ecosystem in which you live. Include both living and nonliving things. Add labels for the parts of the ecosystem.

*Drawings should include an outdoor setting that is part of the student's environment. Drawings should also include such living things as animals, plants, and people, and such nonliving things as soil, rocks, water, and sunshine.*

Use your labels in 3–4 sentences to explain how parts of your ecosystem interact.

*Answers will vary but should include at least one example of interaction.*

## My Summary of the Lesson

**Sample answer:**

On Earth, living things interact with each other. Living things need energy and nutrients to stay alive.

# Life's Diversity

## My Word List

**A. Definition Chart** Find these words in the lesson. Write the definition and use each word in a sentence. Use the *ACCESS Science* glossary for help.

| Word | Definition | Example Sentence |
| --- | --- | --- |
| characteristics | differences you can observe | Different kinds of dogs have different characteristics. |
| diversity | differences | There is a lot of diversity in the animal kingdom. |
| classify | arrange or put into groups | Observing characteristics helps you classify something. |
| category | group with similar characteristics | A kingdom is the largest category of living things. |

**B. Sentence Frame** Complete each sentence below using words from the chart above.

1. When I _____classify_____ a living thing, I start by making observations.

2. Every _____category_____ of life has different characteristics.

3. _Characteristics_ include colors and shapes I can observe.

4. Scientists classify living things because of life's great _____diversity_____.

Name _____

FOR USE WITH PAGE 127

**Skill Building**

**A. Make Observations**  Fill in the Classification Organizer to record characteristics of a tree you can observe or imagine. Observe or imagine the tree, and then fill in the Observation column.

| Characteristic | Observation |
|---|---|
| Where it lives | *Answers will vary.* |
| Its color(s) | *Answers will vary.* |
| Unicellular or multicellular? | multicellular |
| How it gets energy | from sun, water, and soil |

**B. Use Signal Words**  Use the details from your organizer to write 3 sentences about why the tree is a member of the plant kingdom. Remember to use signal words, such as *kinds*, *characteristics*, *group*, *category*, and *includes*.

*Sample answer:*

Like other plants, trees respond to light and gravity and can't move from place to place. All trees are multicellular. The plant kingdom includes many living things with these characteristics.

## My Study Notes

**A. Study Skill: Using Classification Notes** Complete these Classification Notes for the lesson. Use headings and details from *ACCESS Science* to fill in the empty parts.

| Kingdom | Cell Type and Number | Other Details |
|---|---|---|
| archaebacteria | prokaryote one | reproduce by splitting in half; live in unusual places |
| eubacteria | prokaryote one | 3 shapes: spheres, rods, spirals |
| protists | eukaryote one or many | 3 groups: producers, consumers, decomposers |
| fungi | eukaryote one or many | decomposers |
| plants | eukaryote many | producers |
| animals | eukaryote many | consumers |

**B. Key Facts** Use the Word Bank to complete these sentences.

1. My __scientific name__ is *Homo sapiens*.
2. A eukaryotic cell has a ____nucleus____, but a prokaryotic cell does not.
3. When cells do different jobs, they are ____specialized____.
4. Living things come in many ____varieties____.
5. I can observe different ____characteristics____ when I look at a living thing.

**Word Bank**
nucleus
characteristics
specialized
varieties
scientific name

## Showing What I Know

**Classifying**   Draw a picture of a living thing you have observed this week. Write the words you need to classify this organism in the Word Bank below. Then tell a partner the characteristics you used to classify the living thing.

*Sample answer:*

**My Word Bank**

*Sample answer:*

multicellular

consumer

eukaryotic

mammal

backbone

# My Summary of the Lesson

*Sample answer:*

Scientists classify living things. Scientists put living things into 6 kingdoms. They group living things by their characteristics.

# Cell Structure

My Word List

**A. Definition Web** Write definitions in the ovals to complete the Definition Web below.

cell

cell cycle

the life cycle of a cell, including resting, growing, and dividing

daughter cells

the two cells that result when a parent cell divides

cell division

the process by which cells make copies of themselves

parent cell

a cell that is going to divide

**B. Writing Sentences** Now write 3–4 sentences describing the steps in the cell cycle. Use words from your Definition Web.

Cells rest, grow, and divide during the cell cycle. Part of the cycle

includes cell division. During cell division, a parent cell divides itself

into two cells. The new cells are called daughter cells.

### Skill Building

**A. Visualize**  Draw a picture in the box to help you visualize an animal cell. Use the diagrams on pages 137 and 141 of *ACCESS Science* to help you.

> *Drawings should show an irregularly shaped cell and a vacuole, a cell membrane, a nucleus, a mitochondrion, and the cytoplasm.*

**B. My Word Bank**  Now write words to describe your picture. Include names for the different parts of the animal cell. Then label your picture.

vacuole

cell membrane

nucleus

mitochondrion

cytoplasm

## My Study Notes

**A.** **Study Skill: Using a Web**  Use the information on pages 140–141 of *ACCESS Science* to complete this Web. Write the job of each cell part in the ovals.

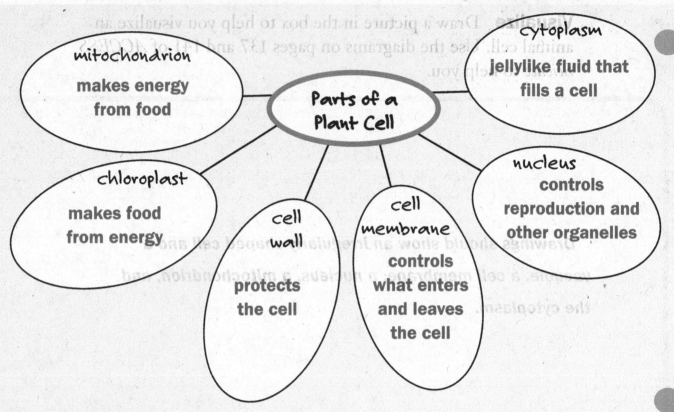

mitochondrion
**makes energy from food**

Parts of a Plant Cell

cytoplasm
**jellylike fluid that fills a cell**

chloroplast
**makes food from energy**

nucleus
**controls reproduction and other organelles**

cell wall
**protects the cell**

cell membrane
**controls what enters and leaves the cell**

**B.** **Key Facts**  After you read the lesson, match each definition with the word it describes. Write the letter of the word on the line.

**1.** __C__  A cell that has a nucleus

**2.** __A__  Parts that do special jobs in eukaryotic cells

**3.** __G__  A disease caused by out-of-control cell division

**4.** __E__  Structures that hold all the information a cell needs to pass on when it divides

**5.** __B__  How plants use sunlight to make food

**6.** __D__  The set of stages in the division of a cell's nucleus

**7.** __F__  How cells copy themselves

**Word Bank**
A. organelles
B. photosynthesis
C. eukaryotic
D. mitosis
E. chromosomes
F. cell division
G. cancer

**Showing What I Know**

**A. Comparing and Contrasting** Use the Venn Diagram to compare and contrast animal cells and plant cells.

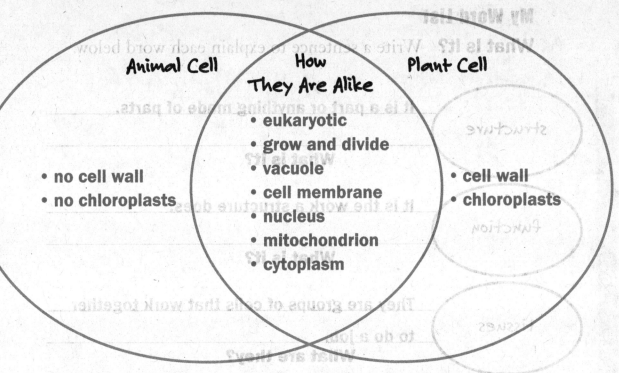

Animal Cell

How They Are Alike

Plant Cell

- no cell wall
- no chloroplasts

- eukaryotic
- grow and divide
- vacuole
- cell membrane
- nucleus
- mitochondrion
- cytoplasm

- cell wall
- chloroplasts

**B. Writing Sentences** Write 3–4 sentences telling how animal cells and plant cells are alike and different. Use the details in your Venn Diagram.

Animal cells and plant cells are both eukaryotic. They have

many of the same kinds of organelles. Only plant cells have

chloroplasts and cell walls.

# My Summary of the Lesson

**Sample answer:**

Cells do jobs. Organelles are special parts of cells. Cells copy
themselves through cell division.

**Name** _____

# Cells to Organisms

## My Word List

**A. What Is It?** Write a sentence to explain each word below.

**structure** — It is a part or anything made of parts.
**What is it?**

**function** — It is the work a structure does.
**What is it?**

**tissues** — They are groups of cells that work together to do a job.
**What are they?**

**organs** — They are structures made of specialized tissues that do specific jobs.
**What are they?**

**organ systems** — They are groups of organs that work together.
**What are they?**

**B. Completing a Paragraph** Use the words above to complete the paragraph below.

From cells to organ systems, each part of your body is a _**structure**_. Each of these has a different job, or _**function**_. The smallest part of your body is a cell. Cells work together in _**tissues**_. Different tissues make up _**organs**_. Different organs work together in _**organ systems**_.

### Skill Building

**A. Organize Data**   Use information from page 153 of *ACCESS Science* to fill in this Size Organizer about muscles. Put the parts in order from smallest to largest.

muscular system      skeletal muscle fiber      skeletal muscle bundle      leg muscle

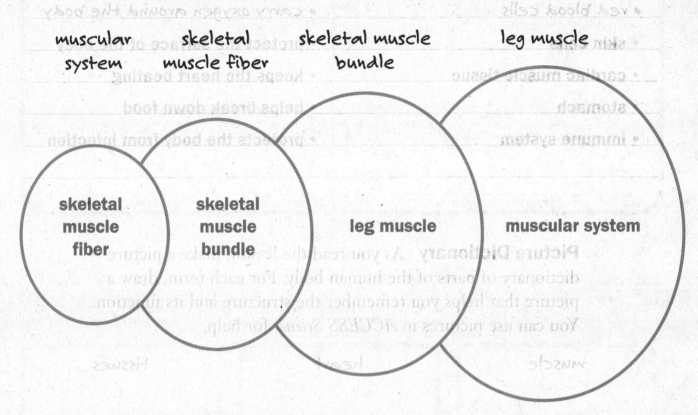

skeletal muscle fiber    skeletal muscle bundle    leg muscle    muscular system

**B. Writing Sentences**   Use the details from your organizer to write 2–3 sentences telling how these parts of the muscular system are related.

Skeletal muscle fibers are cells that work together in bundles.

Bundles of fibers make up a muscle, such as a leg muscle. Leg

muscles and all other muscles are part of the muscular system.

## My Study Notes

**A.** **Study Skill: Using a Two-column Chart**   Complete a Two-column Chart for this lesson. Write body structures in the left column. Write their functions in the right column. Include examples of cells, tissues, organs, and organ systems.   *Sample answer:*

| Structure | Function |
|---|---|
| • red blood cells | • carry oxygen around the body |
| • skin cells | • protect the surface of the body |
| • cardiac muscle tissue | • keeps the heart beating |
| • stomach | • helps break down food |
| • immune system | • protects the body from infection |
|  |  |

**B.** **Picture Dictionary**   As you read the lesson, make a picture dictionary of parts of the human body. For each term, draw a picture that helps you remember the structure and its function. You can use pictures in *ACCESS Science* for help.

| muscle | heart | tissues |
|---|---|---|
| Answers will vary. | | |

| blood vessels | circulatory system | digestive system |
|---|---|---|

**Showing What I Know**

**Describing** Think of a structure in your body that you learned about in this lesson. Or think of a structure that is part of your everyday life, such as a bicycle or a house. Fill in the Size Organizer to show the parts of the structure from smallest to largest. Write the name of your structure in the bottom section of the organizer.

*Sample answer:*

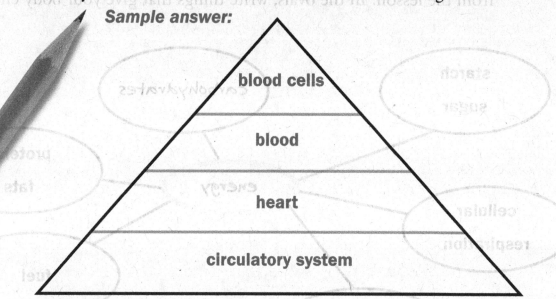

blood cells

blood

heart

circulatory system

Write 3–4 sentences describing how the parts of your structure work together. Use the details from your Size Organizer.

*Sample answer:*

**Many cells make up blood. Blood moves through the heart. The heart pumps blood around the body through the circulatory system.**

# My Summary of the Lesson

*Sample answer:*

**Living things are made of parts that work together. The parts are structures, and the jobs they do are functions.**

# Energy and Nutrients

**My Word List**

**A. Word Web** Complete the Word Web below with vocabulary words from the lesson. In the ovals, write things that give your body energy.

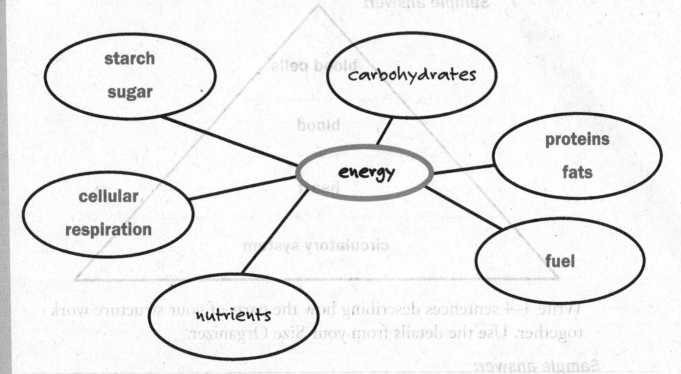

starch
sugar

carbohydrates

proteins
fats

cellular respiration

energy

fuel

nutrients

**B. Drawing and Writing** In the space below, draw a picture of a food you think gives your body energy. Then on the lines write 3–4 sentences about your picture. Use at least 3 words from your Word Web.

Sample drawing:

apple

_Sample answer:_

An apple is a fruit. Fruits have sugar. Sugar is a nutrient that gives you quick energy. Sugar is a kind of carbohydrate. In cellular respiration, cells break down sugar and release energy.

**Skill Building**

**A. Use Math** Complete this chart to show how many daily Calories should come from each nutrient for teen girls and boys. Multiply the total recommended Calories by the percent for each nutrient. For example, 2,200 × 30% = 2,200 × 0.30 = 660 daily Calories from fat for a teen girl.

| Nutrient | Percent of Daily Calories Needed | Recommended Calories: Teen Girl | Recommended Calories: Teen Boy |
|---|---|---|---|
| Carbohydrates | 60 | 1,320 | 1,680 |
| Fats | 30 | 660 | 840 |
| Proteins | 10 | 220 | 280 |
| Total | 100 | 2,200 | 2,800 |

**B. Writing Sentences** Use the details from your chart to write 2–3 sentences about your own daily Calorie needs. Which nutrient should you eat to get most of your Calories?

*Sample answer:*

As a teen boy, I should get about 2,800 Calories each day. More than half of my Calories should come from carbohydrates. I need some Calories from fats, but not too many. Less than a third of my Calories should come from fats.

## My Study Notes

**A. Study Skill: Using Key Word or Topic Notes** Use the information under the red headings in *ACCESS Science* to complete the Key Word or Topic Notes below. Write notes about each topic in the second column.

| Key Words or Topics | Notes |
|---|---|
| Turning Energy into Food | Plants use energy from the sun, carbon dioxide, and water to make food during photosynthesis. Plants make sugar molecules in the chloroplasts of leaf cells. |
| How to Turn Food into Energy | Living things need energy. Cells turn food into energy during cellular respiration. Cells need sugar and oxygen for cellular respiration. Mitochondria in cells turn sugar and oxygen into energy. |
| What Are Nutrients? | Food gives you nutrients. Four main groups of nutrients are: carbohydrates, fats, proteins, and vitamins and minerals. The food pyramid shows how many servings you need to eat from each food group. |

**B. Key Facts** As you read the lesson, use the Word Bank to match each sentence with the word it describes. Write the letter of the word on the line.

**Word Bank**
A. calcium
B. cellular respiration
C. minerals
D. vitamins

1. __A__ Milk and cheese contain this bone-building mineral.

2. __B__ In this process, cells break down food to make energy.

3. __D__ These nutrients help cells do their jobs. They contain carbon.

4. __C__ These nutrients help support your body's structures.

FOR USE WITH PAGE 170

## Showing What I Know

**A. Interpreting**  Study these food labels for different snacks. On each label, find and circle the grams and the percent Daily Value of total fat. Then do the same for total carbohydrate, using boxes instead of circles. Which snack do you think is better for your body?

| **Nutrition Facts** | |
|---|---|
| Serving Size 3 cookies (26 g) | |
| Servings Per Container 6 | |
| **Amount Per Serving** | |
| **Calories** 100   Calories from Fat 20 | |
| | % Daily Value |
| **Total Fat** (2 g) | (3%) |
| Saturated Fat 0 g | |
| **Cholesterol** 0 mg | 0% |
| **Sodium** 170 mg | 7% |
| **Total Carbohydrate** (20 g) | (7%) |
| Dietary Fiber Less than 1 g | 3% |
| Sugars 9 g | |
| **Protein** 1 g | |

| **Nutrition Facts** | |
|---|---|
| Serving Size 18 puffs (28 g) | |
| Servings Per Container 4.5 | |
| **Amount Per Serving** | |
| **Calories** 130   Calories from Fat 60 | |
| | % Daily Value |
| **Total Fat** (6 g) | (10%) |
| Saturated Fat 1 g | |
| **Cholesterol** 0 mg | 0% |
| **Sodium** 150 mg | 5% |
| **Total Carbohydrate** (17 g) | (6%) |
| Dietary Fiber 2 g | 8% |
| Sugars 1 g | |
| **Protein** 2 g | |

**B. Writing Sentences**  Write 3–4 sentences explaining your snack choice.

_Sample answer:_

I chose the cookies because they have less fat than the puffs. The cookies also have fewer Calories. The puffs have more fiber and less sodium, which is good, but I am trying to eat less fat.

# My Summary of the Lesson

_Sample answer:_

Living things need nutrients for energy. Food has nutrients that give living things energy.

© GREAT SOURCE. ALL RIGHTS RESERVED.

LESSON 13 • ENERGY AND NUTRIENTS  **57**

# Responding to the Environment

### My Word List

**A. Definition Chart** Find these words in the lesson. Write the definition and use each word in a sentence.

| Word | Definition | Example Sentence |
|---|---|---|
| equilibrium | state of balance | When I sweat a lot, I drink water to maintain equilibrium. |
| senses | the ways the body gets information about the environment | Sight and hearing are two senses to use while driving a car. |
| stimulus | something an organism can sense | The pain from touching a hot pan on the stove is a strong stimulus. |
| response | the reaction to a stimulus | My response to touching a hot pan is moving my hand away quickly. |
| reflexes | automatic responses to a stimulus | Reflexes help you move quickly in an emergency. |

**B. Choosing Vocabulary** Read each sentence below. Then underline the word that best completes each sentence.

1. My body's (<u>reflexes</u>, response) happen so fast that I don't think about them.

2. All living things work to stay in balance, or maintain (<u>equilibrium</u>, stimulus).

3. (Reflexes, <u>Senses</u>) include sight, hearing, smell, taste, and touch.

4. Feeling hungry might be a (<u>response</u>, reflexes) to the smell of good food.

5. Bright sunlight is a (senses, <u>stimulus</u>) that might cause you to squint.

Name

## Skill Building

**A. Use the Science Process** Think about stimuli in your home, such as smells from the kitchen, the indoor temperature, and sounds outside the window. Write 3 possible stimuli in the first column below. In the second column, predict your response to each stimulus.

*Sample answer:*

| Stimulus: *If* | Response: *Then* |
| --- | --- |
| If it gets very cold, | then I will shiver. |
| If I hear the alarm clock, | then I will wake up. |
| If I peel an onion, | then I will get tears in my eyes. |

**B. Writing Sentences** Write 2–3 sentences telling how you might test your predictions.

*Sample answer:*

I could step outside on a cold day to see if I shiver. I could set the alarm clock to see if I wake up when it goes off. I could peel an onion to see if it makes me get tears in my eyes.

## My Study Notes

### A. Study Skill: Outlining the Lesson  Complete a study outline of this lesson. Use the headings in *ACCESS Science* to fill in the blanks.

1. Responding to the Inside Environment
   a. Balancing Temperature
   b. **Balancing Fluid Levels**
   c. **Balancing Energy**
   d. **Balancing Chemical Levels**
2. Responding to the Outside Environment
   a. **Organisms and Light**
   b. Reflexes
   c. **How the Nervous System Works**
3. **Defending the Body**
   a. The First Defense
   b. **Infections**
   c. **The Second Defense**

### B. Key Facts  As you study the lesson, use the Word Bank to complete these sentences.

| Word Bank |
| --- |
| nervous system |
| infection |
| immune system |
| glands |

1. Your _____glands_____ make chemicals and send them to other parts of your body that use them.

2. Your _____nervous system_____ is made up of your brain, spinal cord, nerves, and sense organs.

3. Your body's _____immune system_____ protects it from germs and viruses.

4. When germs and viruses get into your body, they can cause _____infection_____.

Name

Name

Name

**Name**

**Name**

## Showing What I Know

**A. Predicting** Think about an outdoor activity or sport you enjoy. In the first box, draw a picture of a stimulus that might occur, such as the sounds and actions of other people or animals in the environment. In the second box, draw a picture to show how your body might respond to the stimulus.

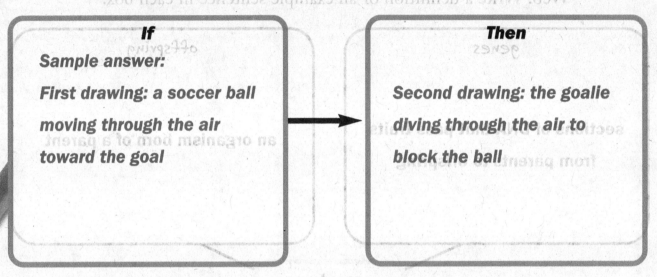

**If**

Sample answer:

First drawing: a soccer ball moving through the air toward the goal

**Then**

Second drawing: the goalie diving through the air to block the ball

**B. My Word Bank** Write words on the lines below to describe your pictures. Then explain your prediction to a partner.

Sample answer:

moving ball
blocking ball
stimulus
response

The ball moving toward the goal is a stimulus. The response of the goalie is to move to block the ball.

## My Summary of the Lesson

Sample answer:

Living things respond to stimuli in the environment. Living things also defend themselves against infection.

# Reproduction and Inheritance

**My Word List**

**A. Definition Web** As you study the lesson, complete this Definition Web. Write a definition or an example sentence in each box.

**genes**

sections of DNA that pass traits from parents to offspring

**offspring**

an organism born of a parent

**reproduce**

**traits**

characteristics that can be controlled by genes

**inherit**

receive a set of traits from one or more parents

**B. Sentence Frame** Use the words in your Definition Web to complete the paragraph below.

Living things __reproduce__ to create babies. Parents' babies are called their __offspring__. Each parent has chromosomes that carry __genes__. These determine what __traits__ the offspring will have. That's how children __inherit__ traits from their parents.

**Name** _____

**Skill Building**

**A. Look for Patterns** In the box below, draw a picture of the people in your family or a family you know. Include brothers and sisters, parents, and grandparents. Show details such as hair and eye color. Then look at your picture. What traits do the family members have? Do you see a pattern?

*Answers will vary.*

**B. My Word Bank** First, use details from your picture to write the words you need to describe your pattern of family traits. Then, explain your pattern to a partner.

*Answers will vary.*

_____   _____

_____   _____

_____   _____

Name _____

**My Study Notes**

**A. Study Skill: Using a Magnet Summary** Complete a Magnet Summary for this lesson. Use headings in the book to fill in the detail boxes. Then write a short summary about the topic.

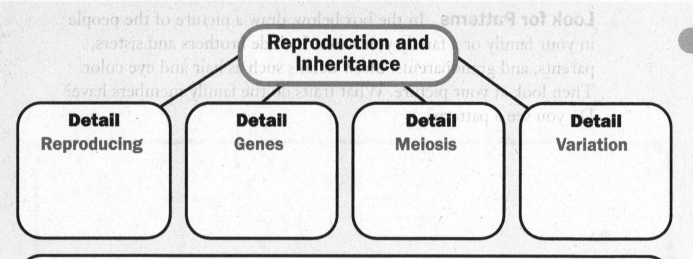

**My Summary**

*Sample answer:*

Reproducing passes genes from parents to offspring. Meiosis produces sex cells that carry genes. Variation comes from new combinations of genes in the sex cells.

**B. Key Facts** Use the Word Bank to complete these sentences.

1. When there is only one parent, the offspring is produced ___**asexually**___.

2. When two parents create offspring together, it is done through ___**sexual**___ reproduction.

3. Sex cells are created in a process called ___**meiosis**___.

4. When a ___**dominant gene**___ is present, the offspring will have the trait it carries.

5. An offspring can have a recessive trait only if it inherits a ___**recessive gene**___ from each parent.

**Word Bank**
meiosis
recessive gene
sexual
dominant gene
asexually

**Name** _____

## Showing What I Know

**A. Describing**   In the Punnett squares below, B stands for the dominant gene of brown eyes and b stands for the recessive gene of blue eyes. Write letters in the squares on the left to show all the possible combinations. Then draw and color a picture of each child's eyes in the squares on the right. *Drawings should show:*

|   | **B** | **b** |
|---|-------|-------|
| **B** | BB | Bb |
| **b** | Bb | bb |

|   | **B** | **b** |
|---|-------|-------|
| **B** | brown eyes | brown eyes |
| **b** | brown eyes | blue eyes |

**B. Writing Sentences**   Imagine that the parents Bb and Bb have 4 children, one for each square. What color eyes would most of their children have? Explain your answer in 2–3 sentences.

_Sample answer:_

It is likely that most of the children will have brown eyes. That is because most will get a dominant gene. If a child gets two recessive genes, he or she will have blue eyes.

# My Summary of the Lesson

_Sample answer:_

Living things reproduce. The offspring inherit genes from the parents. Genes determine traits in offspring.

# Change over Time

## My Word List

**A. Definition Chart**  Find these words in the lesson. Write the definition and use each word in a sentence.

| Word | Definition | Example Sentence |
|---|---|---|
| adaptation | a change that helps an organism survive and reproduce | Hibernating is an adaptation. |
| advantage | a benefit | Long necks gave some giraffes an advantage. |
| natural selection | the process by which helpful traits pass on to new generations | Natural selection is how species change. |
| generations | groups living at the same time and at the same stage of descent | Four generations live in my house. |
| extinction | disappearance from life | Animals face extinction when they can no longer adapt to their environment. |

**B. Sentence Frame**  Use the words in your Definition Chart to complete the sentences below.

1. When bears developed the _____adaptation_____ of sleeping during the winter, it helped the species survive.

2. Species that do not adapt to their environments over time may face _____extinction_____.

3. Changes in a species develop over many _____generations_____.

4. Insects that blend into their environments can have an _____advantage_____ over insects that do not blend in.

5. The process of _____natural selection_____ is how adaptations pass to new generations of a species.

**Name** _____

### Skill Building

**A. Identify Evidence**  After you read page 201 of *ACCESS Science*, complete this Evidence Organizer to support the hypothesis below. Write evidence that supports the hypothesis in the two boxes.

**Hypothesis:**

Walking stick insects have adaptations that help them survive in their environment.

**Evidence:**

The insect's long, narrow shape makes it look like a stick.

**Evidence:**

The insect's brown coloring helps it look like a stick.

**B. Writing Sentences**  Use the details from your organizer to write 2–3 sentences explaining how your evidence supports the hypothesis.

*Sample answer:*

Walking stick insects are long, narrow, and brown. This makes them look like sticks. Birds do not eat sticks, so the insects are safe from birds.

## My Study Notes

**A. Study Skill: Outlining the Lesson** Complete a study outline of this lesson. Use the headings in *ACCESS Science* on pages 200–205 to fill in the outline.

1. Traits and Adaptations _____

   a. Changing Traits _____

   b. **Changing Behaviors** _____

2. **Survival and Selection** _____

   a. Requirements for Survival _____

   b. **Variations** _____

3. Evidence of Change _____

   a. **Studying Fossils** _____

   b. **Observing Anatomy** _____

**B. Key Facts** Use the Word Bank to match each definition with the word it describes. Write the letter of the word on the line.

1. __B__ Helpful adaptations can improve a species' chances of this.

2. __D__ These remains give scientists clues about how species change.

3. __F__ Examples include a parent, a grandparent, and a great-grandparent.

4. __A__ A snake's tiny pelvis is one example of this.

5. __C__ These are small differences among individuals of the same species.

6. __E__ This verb describes how changes come about over time.

**Word Bank**

A. disappearing trait

B. survival

C. variations

D. fossils

E. develop

F. ancestor

Name

FOR USE WITH PAGE 206

## Showing What I Know

**Summarizing**   Draw pictures in the Evidence Organizer to support the hypothesis below. You can use the pictures on page 198 of *ACCESS Science* for clues. Then use your pictures to write a 2- or 3-sentence summary telling how they support the hypothesis.

**Hypothesis:**

Over time, giraffes adapted to the food source in their habitat.

| Giraffes Then | Giraffes' Food Source | Giraffes Now |
|---|---|---|
| *Answers will vary.* | | |

**Summary:**

Giraffes with short necks could not reach leaves in tall trees. They produced fewer offspring. Giraffes with long necks were able to reach food, so they lived longer and reproduced.

# My Summary of the Lesson

**Sample answer:**

Living things have traits. Habitats change and species adapt. Species that survive pass their traits to the next generation.

# The Structure of Matter

**My Word List**

**A. Definition Web**  Write a definition for each word on the Definition Web. Use pages 210–213 of *ACCESS Science* for help.

**mass:** *Over time giraffes adapted to the food source in their habitat*

the amount of matter in something

**volume:**

the amount of space
something takes up

**matter**

**particles:**

very small pieces of
something

**atoms:**

the smallest parts of something that can be identified

**B. Completing a Paragraph**  Use the words in your Definition Web to complete this paragraph.

Matter is anything that has _____**mass**_____ and takes up space.

Mass is measured in grams. _____**Volume**_____ is measured in cubic

centimeters. All matter is made up of _____**atoms**_____. These

building blocks of matter are made up of even smaller pieces called

_____**particles**_____.

Lesson **17**

**Name** _____

FOR USE WITH PAGE 211

**Skill Building**

**A. Read a Model**  Read this model. Then use the information on pages 213–215 in *ACCESS Science* to write a caption for the model.

**Iron (Fe)**

26P

**Sample answer:**

This atom has 26 protons in its nucleus. It also has 26 electrons. It is a neutral atom of the element iron.

**B. Writing Steps**  Review page 211 in *ACCESS Science*. What steps should you follow when reading a model? Write them here.

Step 1:  **Read the title to learn what the model is about.**

Step 2:  **Look at the labels.**

Step 3:  **Look at how the parts are related.**

Step 4:  **Think aloud. Explain what the model shows.**

© GREAT SOURCE. ALL RIGHTS RESERVED.

LESSON 17 • THE STRUCTURE OF MATTER    **71**

## My Study Notes

**A. Study Skill: Key Word or Topic Notes** Use the information on pages 215–217 of *ACCESS Science* to help you complete these Key Word or Topic Notes. **Sample answer:**

| Key Words or Topics | Notes |
|---|---|
| element | • **A substance made of only one kind of atom** <br><br> • **Its characteristics are called properties.** <br><br> • **Scientists use letter symbols for element names.** |
| molecule | • **A combination of two or more atoms** <br><br> • **Scientists use models to show molecules.** |
| compound | • **A combination of elements in a chemical reaction** <br><br> • **Examples: water, sugar, salt, gasoline** |
| mixture | • **Something made from two or more substances with no chemical reaction** <br><br> • **Can be separated physically** |

**B. Key Facts** As you study the lesson, use the Word Bank to answer these questions.

**Word Bank**
protons
electrons
neutrons
positive
negative

**1.** What kind of charge do electrons have?

_____ **negative** _____

**2.** What particles make up the nucleus of an atom?

__ **protons** __ and __ **neutrons** __

**3.** What kind of charge does the nucleus have?

_____ **positive** _____

**4.** What moves in clouds around the nucleus? _____ **electrons** _____

**Showing What I Know**

**A. Interpreting** Look at the model of the atom below. Count the number of protons and electrons it has. Write the numbers on the lines. Think about what these numbers mean.

**Sodium (Na)**

<u>11</u>  **P**

<u>11</u>  **E**

**B. Writing an Interpretation** In 2–3 sentences, tell what the model above means.

This atom has 11 protons and 11 electrons. The atom is

neutral because it has the same number of positive and

negative charges.

# My Summary of the Lesson

*Sample answer:*

Matter is anything that has mass and takes up space. Matter is made

of atoms. Atoms in matter combine to form molecules and compounds.

# States of Matter

## My Word List

**A. Definition Chart**  Find these words in the lesson. Write the definition and use each word in a sentence.

| Word | Definition | Examples |
|------|------------|----------|
| solid | a state of matter with a definite shape and volume | potato<br>tree<br>rock |
| liquid | a state of matter with a definite volume but no definite shape | broth<br>ocean<br>blood |
| gas | a state of matter with no definite shape or volume | steam<br>air<br>natural gas |

**B. Analyzing a Recipe**  Study the recipe ingredients below. Then make a check mark to show whether each ingredient is liquid or solid.

| Ingredient | Liquid | Solid |
|------------|--------|-------|
| cream | ✓ | |
| mushrooms | | ✓ |
| onion | | ✓ |
| water | ✓ | |
| salt | | ✓ |

### Skill Building

**A. Visualize** Draw a picture that shows the 3 states of matter.

> *Answers will vary. If students show particles, be sure that*
> *solids are most densely packed.*

**B. Writing Sentences** Now write 2–3 sentences that say how your picture shows 3 different states of matter.

*Answers will vary.*

_____

_____

_____

_____

_____

_____

**My Study Notes**

### A. Study Skill: Main Idea Organizer   Use what you've learned in the lesson to complete this organizer. *Sample answer:*

**Main Idea:** A change in the amount of thermal energy can cause matter to change from one state to another.

| Detail | Detail | Detail |
|---|---|---|
| Matter undergoes physical changes. | A change in temperature is a change in thermal energy. | Matter can change state in 5 ways. |
|  |  |  |
|  |  |  |
|  |  |  |

### B. Key Facts   After you study the lesson, choose the word from the Word Bank that matches each definition.

1. _____temperature_____ : a measure of the average kinetic energy of a substance

2. _____weight_____ : the measure of the force of gravity on an object's mass

3. _____condense_____ : turn from a gas to a liquid

4. _____density_____ : mass per unit volume

5. _____classify_____ : sort or organize by characteristics

**Word Bank**

weight

temperature

classify

density

condense

Name

## Showing What I Know

**Describing**   Complete these Summary Notes by describing each kind of change. Use pages 224–229 of *ACCESS Science* if you need help.

| | |
|---|---|
| **Topic:** | How matter can change state |
| **Main Point:** | Matter can change state in 5 ways. |

1. Solid to liquid: **If thermal energy is added to a solid, the particles in the solid move faster and farther apart. The particles move fast enough that they are no longer locked together, and the solid melts into a liquid.**

2. Liquid to solid: **When a liquid cools, the particles slow down. Particles lock together when a liquid freezes and turns into a solid.**

3. Liquid to gas: **When enough thermal energy is added to a liquid, it boils. The particles move very fast. When they move far apart, the liquid turns into a gas.**

4. Gas to liquid: **When a gas cools, thermal energy leaves the gas. The particles condense to form a liquid.**

5. Solid to gas: **Some solids turn directly into a gas without becoming a liquid. This is sublimation.**

## My Summary of the Lesson

*Sample answer:*

   **The 3 states of matter are solid, liquid, and gas. Atoms are always moving. All matter has physical properties.**

# Properties and the Periodic Table

**My Word List**

**A. Word Match** Match each vocabulary word in Column 1 to the most closely related meaning in Column 2. Put the letter of the best meaning in Column 2 on the line in Column 1.

| Column 1 | Column 2 |
|---|---|
| element __B__ | A. unique |
| react __D__ | B. substance |
| nucleus __E__ | C. characteristics |
| stable __F__ | D. change |
| properties __C__ | E. center |
| distinctive __A__ | F. balanced |

**B. Writing Sentences** Use some words from Column 1 above to write two sentences. The first sentence should explain the term *properties*, and the second sentence should tell about the periodic table.

*Sample answer:*

**Sentence 1** __Distinctive properties are characteristics that make__

__one element different from other elements.__

**Sentence 2** __The periodic table is a chart that organizes elements__

__by their properties.__

## Skill Building

**A. Ask Questions** Work with a partner. Each of you should choose a classroom object without telling the other what it is. Then think of yes/no questions you can ask your partner to figure out what object he or she chose. Write your questions below. Then ask your partner the questions. Answer your partner's questions.

**Is it smaller than my hand?**

**Is it bendable?**

**Is it soft or hard?**

**Does it conduct heat?**

**Is it heavier than my textbook?**

*(Actual questions will vary. Check for proper question form.)*

**B. Writing a Description** Write a description of your partner's object. Tell as many of its properties as you can.

*Answers will vary.*

## My Study Notes

### A. Study Skill: Making a Table   Use the periodic table (pages 238–239 in *ACCESS Science*) to complete this chart.

| Element Name | Atomic Number | Chemical Symbol | Metal or Nonmetal? |
|---|---|---|---|
| copper | 29 | Cu | metal |
| potassium | 19 | K | metal |
| calcium | 20 | Ca | metal |
| helium | 2 | He | nonmetal |
| radon | 86 | Rn | nonmetal |

### B. Key Facts   After you study the lesson, use what you learned to answer these questions. Use pages 236–241 in *ACCESS Science* if you need help.

**1.** What is the name of the chart that organizes elements by their properties?

the periodic table

**2.** What are two examples of noble gases (Group 18)?

helium, neon, argon, krypton, xenon, radon, ununoctium

**3.** What are two radioactive elements?

radon, radium, polonium, and elements in the bottom row

**4.** Which group of elements are the best conductors?

the metals

**5.** Which elements are in Period 1?

hydrogen and helium

**Showing What I Know**

**Classifying** Write properties of each group on the chart. Then give one example of each. *Sample answer:*

### Classification

| Metals | Metalloids | Nonmetals |
|---|---|---|
| • shiny<br><br>• bendable<br><br>• conduct heat and electricity | • poor conductors of heat and electricity<br><br>• have properties of metals and nonmetals<br><br>• have higher atomic numbers than metals | • not shiny<br><br>• easy to break<br><br>• do not conduct heat and electricity |
| **Example:**<br>copper,<br>other metals | **Example:**<br>silicon,<br>other metalloids | **Example:**<br>chlorine,<br>other nonmetals |

# My Summary of the Lesson

*Sample answer:*

Each element is different from the other elements. Elements have physical properties. The periodic table is a chart of the elements.

# Bonds, Reactions, and Energy

## My Word List

**A. Paraphrasing Definitions** Look in *ACCESS Science* for the definitions of the terms in Column 1. Then write the definitions in your own words.

| Word | Definition |
|---|---|
| reactant | a substance that reacts with another substance in a chemical reaction |
| product | the result of a chemical reaction |
| energy | the power to make something change |
| compound | a combination of two or more elements that cannot be separated |
| dissolving | breaking up |
| kinetic energy | the energy of movement |

**B. Writing a Definition** After you study the lesson, use the terms *atoms* and *electrons* in your own definition of a *covalent bond*. Then draw a picture of a covalent bond.

| A covalent bond is | My picture |
|---|---|
| a bond where there is the sharing of electrons between atoms | Pictures should show at least one shared electron holding atoms together. |

**Skill Building**

**A. Infer from Evidence**   Reread page 247 in *ACCESS Science*. Visualize a cook cracking open an egg and pouring its contents into a hot pan. Then complete this chart.

| Changes I Observe | What I Already Know | My Inferences About What Happens |
|---|---|---|
| • The runny egg becomes solid.<br>• The sides curl up from the heat.<br>• The yolk becomes lighter in color. | *Answers will vary.* | Heat causes the molecules in the egg to combine to form new bonds. This changes how the egg looks, smells, and tastes. |

**B. Making Notes**   In the boxes, write clues—evidence—that can help you detect a chemical change.

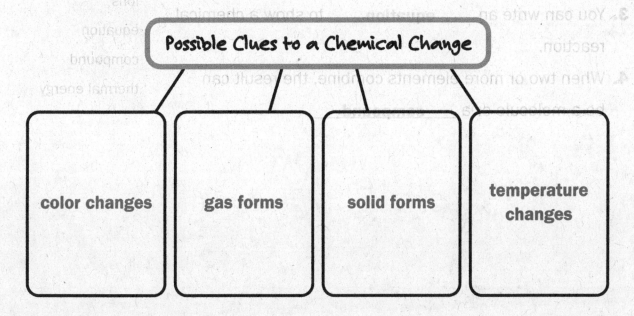

Possible Clues to a Chemical Change

color changes | gas forms | solid forms | temperature changes

## My Study Notes

**A. Study Skill: Outlining the Lesson**  Complete a study outline of Lesson 20. Use the headings in *ACCESS Science* to fill in the blanks.

1. Forming Bonds
    a. Covalent Bonds
    b. **Metallic Bonds**
    c. **Ionic Bonds**
2. Chemical Reactions
    a. **Reactants and Products**
    b. **Equations**
    c. **Conservation of Mass**
3. **Energy in Reactions**
    a. Thermal Energy and Reactions
    b. **Conservation of Energy**

**B. Key Facts**  As you study the lesson, use the Word Bank to complete these sentences.

1. Reactions that release __thermal energy__ are exothermic.

2. Atoms that have a charge are called _____ions_____.

3. You can write an ____equation____ to show a chemical reaction.

4. When two or more elements combine, the result can be a molecule or a ____compound____.

**Word Bank**

ions

equation

compound

thermal energy

## Showing What I Know

**Explaining** Below is an equation for the formation of glucose (sugar). Read it several times and then use the chart to explain the equation in your own words.

| Equation: | $6\ CO_2$ | + | $6\ H_2O$ | → | $C_6H_{12}O_6$ | + | $6\ O_2$ |
|---|---|---|---|---|---|---|---|
| **Explanation words** | 6 molecules of carbon dioxide | plus | 6 molecules of water | make | 1 molecule of glucose | plus | 6 molecules of oxygen |

**Explanation sentence:** 6 molecules of carbon dioxide react with 6 molecules of water to make 1 molecule of glucose plus 6 molecules of oxygen.

Use the formula for glucose to explain conservation of mass.

Conservation of mass means that the total amount of mass is the same before and after a chemical reaction. The products contain the same number of each kind of atom as the reactants: 6 carbon atoms, 12 hydrogen atoms, and 18 oxygen atoms.

## My Summary of the Lesson

**Sample answer:**

When atoms bond, they form molecules. Atoms bond when they share or exchange electrons. When bonds form or break, a chemical reaction happens.

# Understanding Energy

## My Word List

**A. Writing Sentences**  After you study the lesson, use each word below in a sentence about energy. *Sample answer:*

| Word | My Sentence |
|---|---|
| heat | Heat is a movement of thermal energy. |
| radiation | Some moving energy is called radiation. |
| appliance | My favorite appliance that uses electrical energy is my CD player. |
| forms | There are many different forms of energy. |
| motion | Soccer players in motion have kinetic energy. |

**B. Illustrating a Concept**  Visualize a game you like to play outdoors. Then in the first box, draw a picture that shows one or more players with potential energy. In the second box, draw a picture that shows one or more players using kinetic energy.

| Potential energy | Kinetic energy |
|---|---|
| *Actual pictures will vary, but players should be stationary.* | *Players should be moving.* |

**Skill Building**

**A.** **Think About Systems**  Think about standing in a line to get lunch. Assume that this is a system. Read these individual parts of the system. Then put them in an order that makes sense.

Lunch Line System

- Cafeteria workers put food on trays.
- Students make their choices.
- Students pick up their trays.
- Students pay at the cash register.
- Students line up.

1. **Students line up.**
2. **Students pick up their trays.**
3. **Students make their choices.**
4. **Cafeteria workers put food on trays.**
5. **Students pay at the cash register.**

**B.** **Writing Sentences**  Study the lesson in *ACCESS Science*. Then on the lines below, write 4–6 sentences that tell some ways energy affects parts of the lunch line system.

*Sample answer:*

When students stand in line, they have potential energy. As they move through the lunch line and pay, they have kinetic energy. Food contains chemical energy. Sometimes it contains thermal energy. When a cafeteria worker passes food to a student, the worker uses kinetic energy.

## My Study Notes

**A. Study Skill: Summary Notes** As you study the lesson in *ACCESS Science*, complete these Summary Notes. First, read the topic and the main idea. Then, write 4 details that support the main idea.

**Topic:** Energy

**Main Idea:** Energy can change from one form to another.

**1. Two basic kinds of energy are potential and kinetic.**

**2. Energy can change from potential to kinetic and back again.**

**3. When energy changes form, the total amount of energy stays the same.**

**4. When energy changes form, some thermal energy is usually given off.**

**B. Key Facts** Use the Word Bank to match each definition with the word or concept it describes. Then write the letter on the line. You will not use all the letters.

| Word Bank |
| --- |
| A. transforms |
| B. thermal energy |
| C. motion |
| D. forms |
| E. mechanical energy |
| F. convection |

1. __D__ This noun means different kinds.

2. __F__ The movement of energy through moving liquid or gas

3. __E__ Potential and kinetic energy combined

4. __A__ Changes from one kind to another

5. __B__ An increase in this warms a room.

Name _____

## Showing What I Know

**A. Relating** Imagine writing a report on electricity as a system. On the Web below, place the steps in the ovals in order. Explain how each step in the system relates to the next step. Draw arrows to show the sequence. *Sample answer:*

**Power Plant**
At power plants, coal is burned to release thermal energy.

**Turbines**
The thermal energy heats water, which turns to steam and turns the turbines. This creates kinetic energy.

*electricity*

**Appliances**
Appliances then turn electricity into other forms of energy.

**Power Lines**
Turbines connect to generators to make electricity. Electricity flows through power lines to buildings.

**B. Writing a Paragraph** Write a paragraph that relates the parts of electricity as a system. Pretend you are giving instructions to a new student.

*Answers will vary.*

_____

_____

_____

_____

## My Summary of the Lesson

**Sample answer:**

Energy can change form. When energy changes form, no energy is gained or lost.

FOR USE WITH PAGES 270–277

# Force and Motion

**My Word List**

## A. Defining Terms
After you study the lesson, write a definition for each word below.

<u>velocity</u>  <u>**the combination of speed and direction of motion**</u>

<u>distance</u>  <u>**the amount of space or time between two things**</u>

<u>acceleration</u>  <u>**the change in velocity over a unit of time**</u>

## B. Summarizing Data
Below are data about a roller coaster in Great Heights Park. Study the data, and then summarize how the ride works using the words *velocity*, *distance*, and *acceleration*.

| Roller Coaster: Thrill Rider | |
| --- | --- |
| Length | 2,700 feet |
| Height | 420 feet |
| Drop | 380 feet |
| Speed | 120 mph |
| Acceleration | 0 to 120 mph in 4 seconds |

*Sample answer:*

During a ride on the Thrill Rider, a rider will drop 380 feet!

The distance from beginning to end of the ride is 2,700 feet.

The ride's acceleration, 0 to 120 mph in 4 seconds, is very

fast. The roller coaster probably has twists and turns that

affect its velocity.

**Skill Building**

**A. Ask Questions**  Look at the picture at the top of page 274 in *ACCESS Science* and read the caption. Then imagine you are going to interview a skydiver. What questions would you like to ask? Write 4 questions that relate to the lesson.

**Skydiving Questions**    *Sample answer:*

1. What makes a skydiver fall instead of float after jumping out of a plane?

2. What was the distance of your highest dive?

3. What does it feel like when you release your parachute?

4. What is the hardest part of skydiving?

**B. Science Questions**  After you study the lesson, write 2–4 questions about gravity and friction that you might be able to answer with an experiment.

*Sample answer:*

1. Which force is stronger, Earth's gravity or the force of the wind that helps fly a kite?

2. How steep will a ramp have to be for a quarter to slide down and not be stopped by friction?

3. Which surface causes the most friction, sandpaper or wax paper?

(Actual answers will vary. Check for correct question form.)

## My Study Notes

**A. Study Skill: Visualizing** Choose one of Newton's 3 laws of motion on pages 276–277 in *ACCESS Science* and write it on the lines. Then draw and label a picture that shows the law at work.

_____

*The law chosen will vary.*

_____

_____

*Answers will vary.*

**B. Key Facts** As you study the lesson, list examples in each column of this chart.

*Sample answer:*

| Force | Motion |
|---|---|
| a push or pull | distance and speed |
| gravity | flying |
| friction | Newton's laws |

## Showing What I Know

**Predicting**   Use what you know about Newton's Second Law to predict what will happen when you hit a baseball with a bat. Use the Prediction Organizer below.

| Observations | My Prediction |
|---|---|
| • force of bat against ball | The ball will fly through the air. |
| • push of ball against air | |
| | |
| | |
| | |
| | |

Write 2–3 sentences that explain your prediction.

_Sample answer:_

The force of the bat against the ball will make the ball travel through the air. The harder the swing, the farther the ball will travel.

_____

# My Summary of the Lesson

**Sample answer:**

A force can be a push or a pull. Forces change how things move. Newton was a scientist who studied force and wrote laws about force and motion.

# Light and Sound

My Word List

**A. Understanding Key Concepts** Complete this Web. Define each word and then write a sentence that explains how the word relates to light and sound. *Sample answer:*

Light and Sound

**wave**
A wave is a motion that carries energy through space and time. Both light energy and sound energy travel in waves.

**medium**
A medium is any substance, including solids, liquids, and gases. Sound waves need a medium to move through, but light waves do not.

**B. Writing Sentences** Study the Eyes and Ears illustration at the bottom of pages 282–283 of *ACCESS Science*. Then write 4–6 sentences to explain how our eyes detect light and our ears detect sound.

*Sample answer:*

The lens in the front of the eye focuses light energy on the back of the eye. There the light energy changes into signals. The optic nerve carries the signals to the brain. Sound waves enter the outer ear and go to the eardrum. The eardrum vibrates, which causes little bones to send signals to the brain through a nerve.

## Skill Building

### A. Use Math   Use math to answer these questions. Show your work.

**1.** If light travels at the speed of about 300,000 kilometers per second, how many kilometers does it travel in a half hour?

$300{,}000 \times 60$ **seconds per minute** $\times 30$ **minutes** $= 540{,}000{,}000$ **or 540 million kilometers**

**2.** How many kilometers does it travel in an hour?

$540{,}000{,}000 \times 2 = 1{,}080{,}000{,}000$, **or 1.08 billion kilometers**

**3.** The average distance from Earth to the moon is 384,400 kilometers. How long does it take for light to go from Earth to the moon?

$384{,}400$ **kilometers** $\div 300{,}000$ **kilometers per second** $= 1.28$ **seconds**

### B. Writing Sentences   Use the lines below to write 2–3 sentences that describe the speed of light. Use adjectives and one of the examples above.

*Sample answer:*

**Light travels very quickly. It can go from Earth to the moon faster than I can swallow a large drink of cool water.**

**Name** _____

## My Study Notes

**A.** **Study Skill: Using a Diagram**  After you study Lesson 23 in
*ACCESS Science*, label parts of this diagram using words from the
Word Bank below.

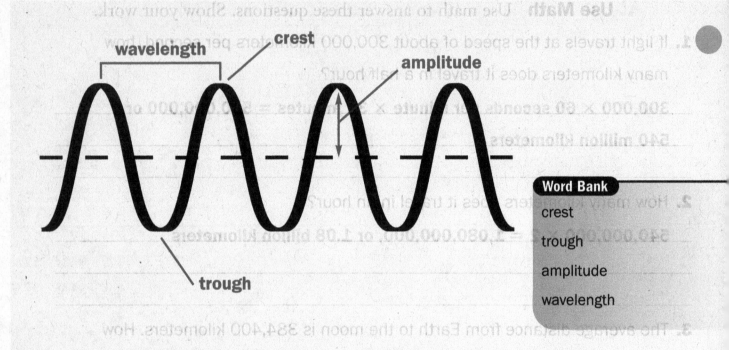

wavelength

crest

amplitude

trough

**Word Bank**

crest

trough

amplitude

wavelength

**B.** **Key Facts**  Study the lesson. Then draw a line between each word
in Column A and the best definition of the word in Column B.

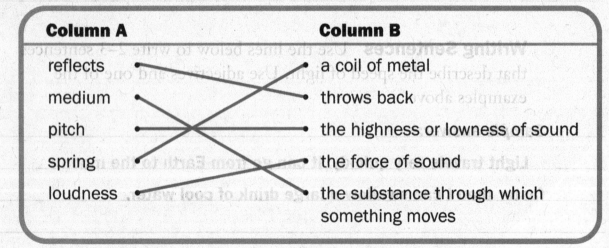

| Column A | Column B |
|----------|----------|
| reflects | a coil of metal |
| medium | throws back |
| pitch | the highness or lowness of sound |
| spring | the force of sound |
| loudness | the substance through which something moves |

## Showing What I Know

**A. Summarizing** Use information from Lesson 23 in *ACCESS Science* to fill in the chart. *Sample answer:*

| Topic | Main Ideas | Summary |
|---|---|---|
| Light waves | • Light waves are called electromagnetic waves.<br><br>• They are part of the electromagnetic spectrum.<br><br>• You can see visible light.<br><br>• Objects may reflect light. | Light waves are called electromagnetic waves. They are a part of the electromagnetic spectrum. Most light comes from the sun. Some of this light reflects off objects. |

**B. Main Ideas** Write three main ideas from the lesson. Then use the list to help as you write your summary of the lesson. *Sample answer:*

1. Light and sound travel in waves.

2. Waves move energy through space and time.

3. Waves interact with matter.

## My Summary of the Lesson

*Sample answer:*

Light and sound travel in waves. Sound needs a medium to travel through. Light does not need a medium.

# Matter in the Universe

## My Word List

**A. Understanding Vocabulary** After you study the lesson, write 2–3 sentences that explain how these three words relate to each other.

| astronomers | galaxies | universe |
| --- | --- | --- |

*Sample answer:*

Astronomers are scientists who study the universe. A part of

what they do is learn about planets and galaxies in outer space.

**B. Writing a Want Ad** Imagine you need to hire an astronomer for a new project. Write an advertisement that tells about the job (a "want ad"). See how many words from the lesson you can use.

*Sample answer:*

Astronomer Needed!

Astronomer needed for a special study of the planets,

stars, galaxies, and moons in our universe. Must be good

with telescopes and all types of space technology.

Contact us by phone or mail.

Name

### Skill Building

**A. Analyze Data** After you study page 295 in *ACCESS Science*, use what you learned to analyze these data. First, read the chart. Then, use a complete sentence to answer each question.

| Planet | Distance from the Sun |
|--------|----------------------|
| Pluto | 5,916,000,000 km |
| Mercury | 57,900,000 km |

Approximately how many times closer is Mercury to the sun than Pluto?

Mercury is about 102 times closer to the sun than Pluto.

How did you find the answer? I divided 5,916,000,000 by 57,900,000.

**B. Comparing Data** Study the data in the chart below. Then compare the diameters and densities of the two planets.

| Planet | Diameter | Density |
|--------|----------|---------|
| Venus | 12,104 km | 5.24 g/cm$^3$ |
| Mars | 6,796 km | 3.93 g/cm$^3$ |

**My Comparisons:**

*Sample answer:*

The diameter of Venus is almost twice the diameter of Mars.

Venus has more grams per cubic centimeters than Mars.

### My Study Notes

**A. Study Skill: Key Word or Topic Notes** As you study Lesson 24 in *ACCESS Science*, complete this chart. Make notes about the following key words or topics.

| Key Words or Topics | Notes |
|---|---|
| universe | contains all matter and energy started with big bang; very large; measured in light-years; includes galaxies |
| stars | held together by gravity make energy through fusion; the sun is a star; made of gas |
| solar system | includes the sun, 9 planets, and moons of the planets; sun holds all planets in their orbits |

**B. Picture Dictionary** Define these two terms. Then draw a picture of an example of each.

gas giant: an outer planet, with no solid surface (Jupiter, Saturn, Uranus, or Neptune)

*Answers will vary.*

terrestrial planet: rocky inner planets (Mercury, Venus, Earth, and Mars)

**Name**

FOR USE WITH PAGE 302

## Showing What I Know

**A. Comparing and Contrasting** Read the data in the chart below. Then use the Venn Diagram to compare and contrast the two planets.

| Planet | Distance from the sun | Number of Moons | Rings? | Diameter |
|--------|----------------------|-----------------|--------|----------|
| Jupiter | 778,330,000 km | 60 | yes | 142,800 km |
| Saturn | 1,429,400,000 km | 31 | yes | 120,000 km |

**Jupiter**
- 778,330,000 km from sun
- 60 moons
- 142,800 km diameter—a little bigger

**Both**
- planet
- gas giant
- have rings

**Saturn**
- 1,429,400,000 km from sun—almost twice as far
- 31 moons
- 120,000 km diameter

**B. Writing Sentences** Write 3 sentences that compare and contrast Jupiter and Saturn.

*Sample answer:*

Both Jupiter and Saturn are gas giant planets with rings.

Jupiter has a larger diameter than Saturn, and it is closer

to the sun. Jupiter has more moons than Saturn.

## My Summary of the Lesson

*Sample answer:*

Earth and the other 8 planets in our solar system are in a galaxy. Galaxies are made of billions of stars, like the sun. The universe is full of galaxies.

# References

## HOW TO MEASURE WITH A METERSTICK

You use a meterstick to measure length. A meterstick is one meter long. It is divided into 100 centimeters. Each centimeter is further divided into ten smaller units called millimeters. You can use all of these units on the meterstick to measure length.

1. Line up the "0" end of the meterstick with one end of the object you are measuring.

2. Look at the other end of the object. Observe how long the object is in centimeters and millimeters.

3. This pencil is 17 centimeters plus 5 millimeters long. You can write this length as 17.5 centimeters.

How do you measure the length of something that is longer than a meter, such as a wall?

1. Line up the "0" end of the meterstick with the end of the wall.

2. Make a light mark on the wall or hold your finger at the other end of the meterstick.

3. Move the meterstick so that the "0" end lines up with the mark or with your finger. Be sure to keep the stick level.

4. Continue to move and mark lengths of the meterstick until you reach the end of the wall. Then add up all the measurements. For example, the wall might be 5 meters and 25 centimeters, or 5.25 meters, long.

# How to Measure Volume

## Volume of a Liquid

The amount of space something takes up is its volume. The water in the large glass takes up more space than the water in the small glass. The pitcher holds a larger volume of water. How much more? You have to measure to find out. In science, you measure volume by using beakers, graduated cylinders, and metric measuring cups. These containers usually are marked in milliliters (mL). The most accurate measuring container is a graduated cylinder.

1. Look at the graduated cylinder. It is marked with 100 mL. Every tenth milliliter is labeled.

2. Pour the liquid you are measuring into a graduated cylinder. Notice that the surface of the water in the cylinder curves up at the sides. You measure the volume by reading the height of the water at the lowest part of the curve. The water shown in the graduated cylinder in the picture has a volume of 65 mL.

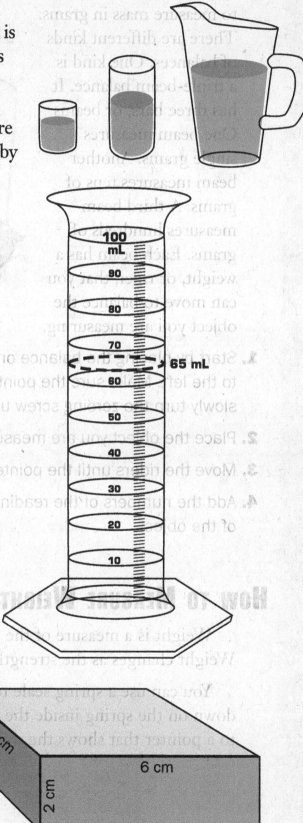

## Volume of a Box

All matter has volume. You can find the volume of a box by multiplying its length by its width by its height. The volume is measured in cubic centimeters (cm³).

volume = length × width × height

   = 6 cm × 3 cm × 2 cm

   = 36 cm³

# How to Measure Mass

You can use a balance to measure mass in grams. There are different kinds of balances. One kind is a triple-beam balance. It has three bars, or beams. One beam measures single grams. Another beam measures tens of grams. A third beam measures hundreds of grams. Each beam has a weight, or rider, that you can move to balance the object you are measuring.

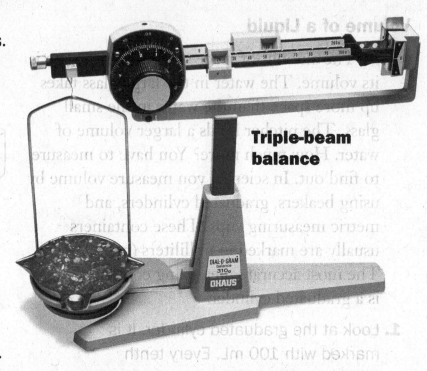

**Triple-beam balance**

1. Start by placing the balance on a level surface. Move the riders all the way to the left. Make sure the pointer points to the zero mark. If it does not, slowly turn the zeroing screw until the pointer is at zero.

2. Place the object you are measuring onto the balance pan.

3. Move the riders until the pointer once again points to the zero mark.

4. Add the numbers of the readings for all three beams. The total is the mass of the object.

# How to Measure Weight

Weight is a measure of the force of gravity on an object's mass. Weight changes as the strength of gravity changes.

You can use a spring scale to measure weight. The object pulls down on the spring inside the plastic tube. The spring is connected to a pointer that shows the weight in newtons (N).

# How to Measure Temperature

Temperature is a measure of thermal energy. You measure temperature with a thermometer.

A thermometer is a narrow tube that contains colored liquid. When a liquid gets warmer, it gains energy. The particles of liquid move farther apart. That makes the liquid rise in the tube. When the liquid gets cooler, it loses energy. The particles move closer together, and the liquid falls in the tube.

1. Look at the thermometer. Notice what scale it uses. The thermometer might use the Fahrenheit scale and measure temperature in degrees Fahrenheit (°F). It might use the Celsius scale and measure in degrees Celsius (°C).

2. Place the thermometer so that the bottom part, or bulb, is in the material you are measuring. For example, when measuring the temperature of water, make sure the bulb is in the water.

3. Wait until the liquid in the thermometer stops moving. This may take a minute or two.

4. Read the number next to the top of the colored liquid. Make sure you know how many degrees each mark on the scale stands for. The temperature shown on this thermometer is 75 °F (23.5 °C).

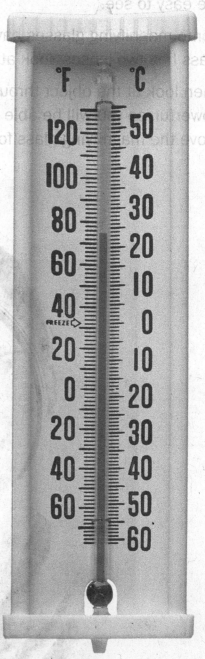

# HOW TO USE A MAGNIFYING GLASS

A magnifying glass is a tool that magnifies an object, or makes the object look bigger. You use a magnifying glass to see details that would be difficult to see without the glass. You might use a magnifying glass to see the shape of a grain of salt. You could use a magnifying glass to observe the legs of an ant or pollen on a flower.

1. Hold the magnifying glass a few centimeters from the object. Move the magnifying glass toward or away from the object until its edges are easy to see.

2. Some magnifying glasses have more than one lens. If your magnifying glass has two lenses, look at the object through the larger lens first.

3. Then look at the object through the smaller lens. This lens is more powerful, so you will be able to see even more detail. You may have to move the magnifying glass forward or away again to see the object clearly.

# How to Use a Microscope

A microscope can make an object look hundreds of times larger. Students often use a kind of microscope called a compound microscope. It has different kinds of lenses.

1. Place the microscope on a flat surface. If you have to carry the microscope, use both hands. Hold the arm of the microscope with one hand and support the base with your other hand.

2. Look at the picture to learn the different parts of the microscope. Take time to find these parts on the microscope you are using.

3. Position the mirror so that it reflects light up toward the stage. Look through the eyepiece. Move the lever of the diaphragm so that the light shines through the opening in the stage.

4. Place a prepared slide on the stage so that the specimen is over the center of the opening. Put the slide under the stage clips to hold the slide in place.

5. Look at the microscope from the side. Turn the coarse adjustment knob to lower the body tube. Lower the tube until the low-power objective almost touches the slide. Do not let the objective touch the slide.

6. Look through the eyepiece. If the object looks blurry, use the coarse adjustment knob to raise the body tube. Make the object appear as clear as you can.

7. Use the fine adjustment knob to make the object appear even more clearly.

8. To change magnification, turn the nosepiece until the high-power objective clicks in place. Then use the fine adjustment knob to make the object appear clearly.

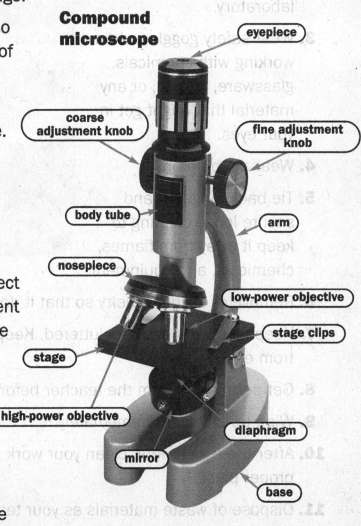

**Compound microscope**

eyepiece

coarse adjustment knob

fine adjustment knob

body tube

arm

nosepiece

low-power objective

stage clips

stage

high-power objective

diaphragm

mirror

base

# Lab Safety

Read these safety rules before doing any science experiment. Ask your teacher to explain any rules you do not understand.

## General Safety

1. Read all of the instructions for an experiment carefully. Ask your teacher to explain any instructions you do not understand. Look for safety symbols and warnings.

2. Never eat or drink in the laboratory.

3. Wear safety goggles when working with chemicals, glassware, flames, or any material that might get in your eyes.

4. Wear a lab apron.

5. Tie back long hair and secure loose clothing to keep it away from flames, chemicals, and equipment.

6. Remove or secure jewelry so that it does not dangle.

7. Keep your work area uncluttered. Keep backpacks and books away from equipment.

8. Get permission from the teacher before beginning any experiment.

9. Wipe up any spills immediately.

10. After the experiment, clean your work area. Return all equipment to its proper place.

11. Dispose of waste materials as your teacher tells you.

12. Wash your hands before leaving the lab.

# Heating and Electrical Safety

**1.** Never heat anything without your teacher's permission.

**2.** Never reach across an open flame.

**3.** Keep any material that can burn, such as nail polish remover, away from flames.

**4.** Never leave a lighted burner or a hot plate unattended.

**5.** When you are heating a substance in a test tube, point the test tube opening away from yourself and others.

**6.** Do not heat a liquid in a closed container.

**7.** Do not touch a burner or hot plate right after you turn it off. It will still be hot. Do not use your bare hands to pick up a container that has just been heated. Find out if it is still hot by holding the back of your hand near it. If you feel heat, use an oven mitt or tongs to pick up the container.

**8.** Never use a piece of electrical equipment that has a frayed cord or an exposed wire.

# Chemical Safety

**1.** Never mix chemicals just to see what happens. Some chemicals that are harmless separately can explode when combined.

**2.** Do not touch, taste, or smell a chemical unless your teacher tells you to do so. If you are instructed to smell a chemical, use a hand motion to waft the odors toward your nose. Never inhale fumes directly from a container.

**3.** When mixing an acid and water, add the acid to the water. Never add water to the acid—it will splatter.

**4.** If you spill or splash a chemical, tell your teacher immediately.

## Glassware Safety

1. Check to make sure heated glassware has cooled before you pick it up with bare hands.

2. Do not eat or drink from lab glassware.

3. Never use broken or chipped glassware, such as chipped microscope slides, beakers, or test tubes.

4. Tell your teacher if glassware breaks. Follow directions for disposing of the broken glassware. Do not handle it with your bare hands.

## Safety with Sharp Objects

1. Handle sharp tools, such as scalpels, knives, pins, and scissors, carefully. Cut by moving the sharp edge away from your body, not toward your body.

2. Tell your teacher if you or someone else gets cut.

3. Cover the edges of cans and other sharp edges with tape.

## Plant and Animal Safety

1. Tell your teacher if you are allergic to any plants or animals.

2. Handle plants or animals as your teacher tells you.

3. Do not taste any part of a plant.

4. Never perform an experiment that will harm an animal.

5. If you keep animals to observe in the lab, learn how to care for them. Keep their homes clean. Give them enough food, water, and space.

6. Wash your hands after handling animals and their cages or tanks. Wash your hands after handling plants or soil.